Ancient Explorers of America

From the Ice Age to Columbus

For Mac

Thanks for all your
help and encouragement

Alech

Solitude Press

Ancient Explorers of America
From the Ice Age to Columbus

ISBN-13   978-1-928874-19-5

Printed in the United States of America

Published by:

Solitude Press
212 Brooks Street
Williamsburg VA 23185

To the Williamsburg Writers Group
for their support, patience, and editorial advice.

And to Ann
for her love and unfailing encouragement

Contents

Foreword

This book recounts many ancient travels by people to the Americas—the New World. What it relates is a story much different from the one that we learned in school. This fascinating tale draws upon genetic science, geography, geology, history, archaeology, anthropology, linguistics, and often upon fragmentary accounts of adventure found in sagas, maritime records, national archives, and other dusty sources.

Nobody knows for certain who the first Americans were. Were they from Asia, as most of us have been taught, or were they from Europe? When did those first people arrive? Did they come before or after the last Ice Age? Most scientists who study this question believe they came after the last Ice Age, but a few tantalizing clues found in both North and South America suggest a much earlier date for the arrival of humans in the Americas. Like so much of the human story, the picture has changed and undoubtedly will change again when new information comes to light and gains acceptance as orthodoxy.

To truly understand the complex cultures that Christopher Columbus incorrectly identified as Indians, we need to know about all the ancient visitors to America who had contact with and may have contributed their genetic material to an expanding American gene pool. The so-called indigenous peoples of the Americas most likely comprised a blending of many cultures from all over the ancient world. They lived in complex societies with well-developed technologies uniquely adapted to their environments and lived in communities that rivaled European cities in size and comfort. Scientists are still unraveling the convoluted genetic history of the native inhabitants who greeted the European explorers in the fifteenth and later centuries.

This book is for general readers, not for academics. The view adopted in this book is that the preponderance of evidence supports the likelihood that various cultures made contact with early America thousands to hundreds of years before Columbus. Most, if not all, of the chapters present controversial material often first advanced by equally controversial proponents; hopefully that makes the story all the more interesting. You will not find footnotes or other scholarly devices to support the stories. This book merely provides a collection of some of the more interesting theories of ancient explorations. It is not intended to convince, only to entertain.

You will find at least one instance where the record is not clear or where a story of contact with America fails the test of reasonableness. The purported American voyage of Sir Henry Sinclair, the Earl of Orkney, has many proponents including descendants of the Earl as well as devotees of the Knights Templar legends. I have included the Sinclair story in Chapter 10, but I encourage readers to make their own decisions on whether Sir Henry made it to America.

The stories occur in roughly chronological order, each chapter focusing on a wave of migration or visit, accidental or intentional, by various cultures. Each chapter presents the documentary record of the journey or voyage, when available, and the artifactual evidence of the presence of those visitors in the New World. Many of these alleged voyages left little trace in the historical record and, as a result, there are both well-respected proponents and opponents within the academic community who debate the validity of these voyages. Legendary writers of early exploration, such as Samuel Eliot Morrison, have derided some stories which have equally well-respected advocates within the academic community.

Professor Barry Fell of Harvard University, one of the most controversial and frequently ridiculed writers on the subject of early contact with the Americas by Phoenicians, Irish, and other cultures, has stimulated a great deal of debate over intriguing linguistic artifacts found in the Americas. Fell and his work on the ancient Ogham form of writing received some vindication not long before his death in 1994 when University of Calgary Professor David Kelley—known for his breakthrough in deciphering Mayan glyphic writing—had this to say about Professor Fell: "Despite my occasional harsh criticism of Fell's treatment of individual inscriptions, it should be recognized that without Fell's work there would be no [North American] Ogham problem to perplex us. We need to ask not only what Fell has done wrong in his epigraphy, but also where we have gone wrong as archaeologists in not recognizing such an extensive European presence in the New World."

Ancient Explorers of America starts with an account of the first people arriving in the New World. The story that begins the first chapter of this book is a fictional account based on the latest scientific theory of who these first people were and where they came from. That theory proposes that people of a culture called Solutrean came across the Atlantic from the Iberian Peninsula at the end of the last Ice Age. This fictional material first appeared in my novel, *Grave Mistakes*. I have included it here in a slightly different form to dramatize the hardships of that first voyage to America and to illustrate how the Solutrean people may have reacted to a promising New World totally lacking in human competition. Subsequent chapters contain less fanciful material extracted from contemporary records and artifacts. I hope you enjoy reading all these stories we never learned in school.

Aleck Loker, Williamsburg, Virginia

Chapter 1
18,000 Years Ago

A ragged band of survivors struggled through the surf and onto the beach. The oarsmen pulled the light boats high up onto the shore and then collapsed onto the fine white sand, soaking up the warmth stored there.

Two months earlier, seventy-five members of the Mananni clan, led by Fein, their headman, had left their old-world homeland in four boats. After weeks coursing westward along the edge of the vast arctic ice sheet, the storm-god Dinn blew up a summer tempest that drove them southwest before a black wall of torrential rain. The howling wind blew the rain straight at their backs, filling their light, skin-covered craft as fast as they could bail out the water. Huge waves, amplified by the storm, propelled them towards the shore like so much flotsam.

Fein felt as fatigued as the rest of the band, but he attended to his duties. Three boats had made it to shore; the fourth had become separated from the others during the storm, and Fein knew there was little hope for survivors. His eldest son, Oisin, commanded that boat, and it contained sixteen others including his son's wife and the infant son she had borne during the voyage. Thank Manan the sea-god that his other two sons had brought their boats safely ashore.

The headman, standing nearly six feet tall—several inches taller than most of the other men—looked at his followers sprawled on the sand and counted their number. Fifty-seven survivors looked to Fein for deliverance from this storm and safe transport into his promised land of plenty. Fein's robust

1

clan members shared the same dark brown hair and stocky build of most of the inhabitants of their land. They varied in age from infants and toddlers to men and women in their late twenties. The latter could not hope for much more than ten more years of life in the mortal world.

The storm continued to howl, and Fein knew that, without shelter, his band could not survive. In spite of their sealskin clothing, they were wet and exhausted from their ordeal and would succumb to the effects of exposure without shelter.

After the oarsmen had rested for a few moments, Fein summoned them and gave them their instructions. Each boat had eight oarsmen. Four men could easily carry one boat, once the passengers and cargo had been removed. Working in two teams, one group of oarsmen emptied a boat and carried the cargo higher up onto the bank. The other team flipped a boat over and carried the upturned craft up the bank, setting it down carefully into the sand with its bow facing into the wind. Then, using their hands, the men dug a tunnel through the sand to make an opening under the boat's gunwale. As soon as they completed the tunnel, the other exhausted travelers crawled under the upturned boat and collapsed again in that makeshift shelter, savoring the tangy odors of the shore and nestling into the comforting sand. Even the young children had no energy to cavort in the security under the boat. They crawled to their mothers and snuggled against them, dropping quickly to sleep.

Soon all three boats lay side by side, upside down, facing the torrent. Some survivors didn't have the strength to walk up the beach and crawl to safety under a boat. The oarsmen carried them the short distance to the relative comfort of the boat shelters. Their stores of dried fish and seal meat had nearly run out, but they had sufficient supplies for everyone to last a day or two.

They couldn't risk lighting a fire, even a seal-oil fire under the boats, because they knew the spirit of the fire would take their breath away in that closed space. However, they remained comfortable because of the body heat trapped under the boats. In spite of the howling wind, nearly every person under those three boats soon fell into a deep sleep.

Fein couldn't sleep. He had instructed the oarsmen to dig the tunnel entrances into the boats on the lee-side to protect them from drifting sand, but he worried that the wind would change direction during the night and their tunnels would be closed. He knew that people had died in sealed caves—he didn't know why, but he knew that always there must be an opening for the spirit of the wind to enter.

He lay awake listening to the wind and the rain drumming on the hide of the boat. Fein mourned the loss of his son and the other clan members who went down with their boat in the storm. He believed that no craft built could have survived that tempest without Manan's protection. Fein wondered why Manan had chosen his son's boat as a sacrifice to appease Dinn, the storm god.

As he lay there he thought about how well those simple boats had withstood all they had encountered. Everyone knew that the Otherworld could be reached across the sea, but no one they knew had ever attempted to travel that far before. Back in their homeland, they built smaller craft to fish along the coast. Those boats seldom exceeded the length of three men lying in a row.

Fein knew they would need larger boats to carry all his clan to the Otherworld. The boats would be the biggest they had ever built—not that it would be much more difficult. They had plenty of solid timber for the frame. The most work would fall to the women to dry, stretch, scrape and stitch many more seal hides together to cover the larger boats. As it turned out, it had taken Fein's clan nearly six moons to build the boats—three times as long as he had anticipated. Their delayed departure meant that they arrived at the Otherworld during the annual storm season at the end of the warm period.

Their choices for the voyage had consisted of two possibilities: they could row west along the vast ice sheet, hunting the abundant sea creatures and animals that lived there; or they could take their chances by rowing south along the coast and hope for another route across the open sea. In the end, the choice seemed obvious. No one had attempted a sea crossing in open water to the south. They had decided to stay with what they knew, coasting along the ice sheet and living, as they had for generations, off of sea birds, seals, and fish inhabiting that arctic region. In a storm, or if a boat became damaged, they could set up camp on the ice sheet. They often did this on shorter hunting expeditions.

Fein wondered if Oisin would still be alive if he had postponed their departure until the next season. But he knew that the longer they remained in their old settlement, the more likely the marauders would have returned.

The boats used by the Solutreans probably resembled the Umiak used well into modern times by the Eskimo people of the Arctic.

After three seasons of their depredations, Fein's clan could not have survived another savage attack by the followers of Bran—the raven clan. The marauders had chosen an appropriate totem; the raven always brought death and destruction. During their last raid, Fein had received a serious wound from a spear thrust into his shoulder, and several men of the band had died in the attack. The raven clan had withdrawn from the raid with nearly all of the Mananni clan's food stores and three of their young women.

The boat frames had been built of strong and resilient yew that could be bent into the arced shape of the hull without cracking. Joints were tied with seal sinews that dried to an incredibly hard bond. The wood would break before the dried sinew let go. Over the wooden framework, they stretched the seal-hide covering as taut as they could draw it.

More sinew fastened the hide to the frame. Where the hide came in contact with the frame, they placed additional seal skin layers, knowing that those spots would wear more quickly as the sea caused the hide to flex against the frame. The women sewed the seams in the hide-covering so tightly that little water could seep through. To further waterproof the hull, they daubed seal tallow onto the seams. By the time the women had completed their job, their already sturdy fingers were so callused in places that they had little or no sense of touch.

The finished boats, twice as long as their usual craft, floated so high on the water that the oarsmen could barely control them in the lightest breeze. But Fein knew that when the passengers and cargo went aboard, the boats would wallow deeper in the water, making them less susceptible to the wind and more controllable. In spite of his confidence, the rest of the clan remained unconvinced until Fein took eight oarsmen, his three sons, and five huge stones aboard for ballast. With one of the boats properly loaded, the oarsmen soon demonstrated to everyone's satisfaction that the boats would serve them well on their voyage across the sea.

Fein's confidence had proven justified during the entire voyage until the last few days. During their voyage along the ice sheet, they had enjoyed relatively good weather. The seas had rolled gently under the light boats and the oarsmen had maintained them on their course. They had spent most nights on the ice sheet sheltered under their boats.

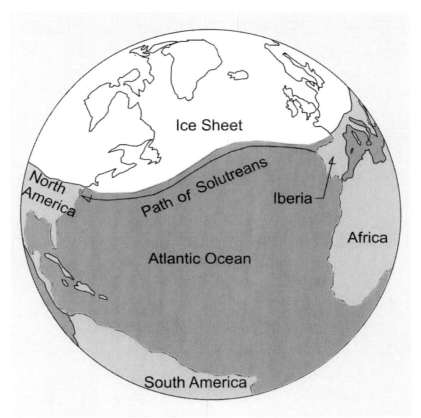

On some particularly calm days when the moon rose fat in the sky, they rowed through the night nearly doubling their daily distance. Whales sounded alongside the little fleet and porpoises came so close they interfered with the rowers' oars. Of the more sinister fiends believed to inhabit the great sea, the Mananni happily saw nothing; however, the women continued to talk about such things and the men told them they were silly, refusing to give voice to their own fears. The children enjoyed the adventure of the voyage and the talk of sea monsters merely added to their delight.

Fish and seals abounded throughout the voyage causing many to question the need to spend time in camp drying the surplus over their fires. But Fein cautioned them that no one could know what Manan or Dinn might throw at them. They needed to keep some dried fish and meat should an emergency beset them as the one that had driven them onto this warm Otherworld shore.

Three days earlier, as they reached the juncture of the ice sheet and the unfrozen shore, the sky grew dark to the south and Fein's damaged shoulder began to ache. He sensed that Dinn had something in store for them. The next day, the seas rolled under the boats more quickly and the boats teetered on the top of the cresting waves before plunging down into the troughs. The oarsmen could not row efficiently because, at times, they were lifted clear of the water by the pitching boats. Fein had to make the difficult decision of whether to draw the boats up onto the ice sheet and take shelter there or to take the boats well away from the jagged edge of the ice to avoid being driven into the ice by the huge waves. He chose to take the boats farther out to sea, putting the ice sheet that could be a refuge or a peril well behind them.

The storm hit. They saw it racing towards them with terrific speed, the rain making an imposing curtain wall that they would have to penetrate. They were caught in an unanticipated combination of sea waves, wind from the northeast, and the rapidly approaching wall of rain. Soon they had all they could do to keep the boats afloat. The passengers bailed furiously to counter the flood of rain, and the oarsmen tried desperately to keep the boats from broaching in the troughs and rolling over.

Oisin's boat took a huge wave broadside that rolled them over. Those who did not have a firm hold fell overboard and quickly disappeared into the roiling seas, their shouts drowned by the howling wind. The brave oarsmen shifted their weight to the high side, and the boat slowly righted itself, but the next wave crashed over it, engulfing everything in a crushing mass of water. Fein lost sight of his son's boat and knew no one could have done anything for them. Each of the remaining boat crews focused on their own survival. It was their only choice.

Now lying on the beach in the safety of the upturned boat, Fein succumbed to sleep. When he awoke hours later, the wind didn't wake him nor did the rain. He awoke to the eerie silence left in the wake of the storm that had veered out into the wide sea.

Fein checked on the welfare of his clan. He found that everyone appeared in much better shape after their sleep. Fortunately none had serious injuries—just a few scrapes and bruises from the battering they took in the storm. He knew from experience that the weather after the storm would be pleasant for at least a few days.

This land they had come to on the ancient shoreline lay well below the margin of the vast ice sheet, in a sub-arctic climate that they considered quite temperate. The forests consisted primarily of conifer trees. Wild game and edible plants abounded. They had reached the land of plenty Fein had promised. And they had left behind them forever the depredations of the marauding, competing clans.

However, Fein did not know that. He thought they had come to the Otherworld—the legendary land of gods and spirits of the dead where their ancestors dwelt. Mortals could only enter the Otherworld by dying or, in rare cases, by divine intervention. The Otherworld provided a life of eternal youth and inexhaustible food and drink. The clan would, in time, discover that they had landed not in the Otherworld but in another part of the mortal world. They would still work hard, experience setbacks, and would grow old and die. That lesson would become apparent to them soon.

Fein roused his clan and prepared them for the next leg of their journey. Once everyone had eaten, they launched their three boats and proceeded south along the coast in search of a river that would give them access to the interior of the land. They rowed all day, making good progress and, since the weather was mild and the moon nearly full, they continued through the night. At dawn, Fein noticed a broad inlet to the west. It was the mouth of a river that, many thousands of years later, the native people would call "Susquehanna." The boats turned and followed the course of that ancient river, rowing against the flow to the sea.

That river bed still exists, but it now lies under the sediment of the Chesapeake Bay and the Atlantic Ocean. The bay would not form until the sea-level had risen enough for the ocean to flood into the ancient river valley and swell out to form the estuary—a process that would not be complete for 15,000 years after Fein's arrival. Five hundred generations of his descendents would witness the transformation of this Sub-Arctic, fresh water, river valley into one of the most productive and largest salt water estuaries in the world.

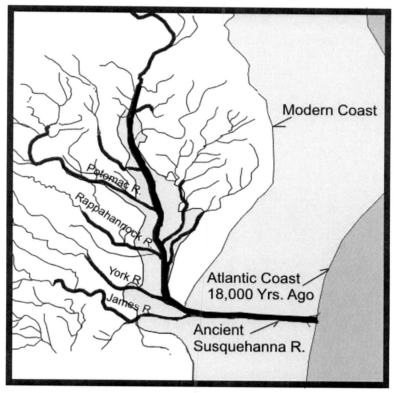

The Mananni clan found plenty to eat on their journey. They caught huge sturgeon as they rowed along. The fish were as big as the largest oarsman, and it took several men to bring them into the boat. When on shore, they also killed deer, rabbit and raccoon. Edible tubers, nuts and green plants rounded out their diets. Being the first humans in this area, they found the wild game relatively easy to catch. Also, they had not come in contact with any animals that posed a threat to them.

Moving up the Susquehanna over the next few days, Fein observed several smaller rivers and streams flowing into the main course from the west. He chose to enter the first large river for no reason other than curiosity. The current flowing down this narrow channel slowed the boats' progress considerably. Fein hoped to locate a favorable spot to establish a permanent settlement. He knew that the cold, fresh water would provide excellent fishing, and the dense forests along the shores would provide the wild game, plants and materials for a successful new home for his clan. He searched for the best spot to camp and also looked for signs of other human inhabitants. He had seen none so far and that greatly puzzled him. He had expected to find many inhabitants in the Otherworld. Perhaps the spirits were invisible. If so, their presence might manifest itself in other ways. Fein kept these thoughts to himself—no sense alarming the other clan members. To secure their good fortune, he resolved to make a suitable offering to Manan when they set up their permanent camp.

After three days rowing up the river, the clan came to a fork formed by two apparently equal branches diverging in nearly opposite directions. Fein chose the left fork and closely studied the land between the branches as they rowed along the shore. The ground seemed level and the bank up from the river high but not too steep a climb. The oarsmen rowed the three boats single file up the left fork for a few miles, where Fein decided, at a bend in the river, that they had found the ideal spot to establish their permanent campsite. The land between the two rivers would provide an excellent base from which they could easily fish in either river, and it would also give them the most defensible position in case there were other clans bent on attack—although he still had seen no sign of other humans.

When Fein announced his decision to settle there, he heard no objections. To the contrary, all the clan members seemed eager to go ashore and set up a permanent camp. None were more eager than the oarsmen—they had clearly carried the heaviest load on this journey. Fein felt great pride in the way his two sons and their crews had borne up under their long journey. He still thought of the son he lost in the storm—the sacrifice to Dinn the storm god that probably saved the rest of the clan. Fein would find a way to ensure that the clan would always remember the sacrifice of Oisin and the others who were lost with him. They would dedicate this place in the Otherworld to his son by calling it the Place of Oisin—meaning the place of the little fawn.

With Fein's direction, the clan beached the boats on a narrow sand spit under the high bank marked by bands of orange and white sand. The Mananni clan's many trips up the bank soon wore a path in the loose cliff material. On the level ground above, they placed their belongings and began the process of laying out their settlement. The huge trees cast broad shadows over the area, and the stunted undergrowth between them was easily cleared by the clan members. They began to select locations for their quarters in the wide areas between the trees. The women laid out a cooking pit and soon the comfort of a warm fire of dead wood gave the campsite a sense of peace and safety that all the clan members had longed for during their voyage across the great sea.

Within days they built shelters and organized the camp around their now numerous cooking hearths. The men killed plenty of deer and small game to supplement the fish they had caught. They told the others how easily they approached the unsuspecting animals of the forest. In their old world, the animals in the woods knew to keep well away from men, but here they seemed unperturbed as the men approached them within close range.

The women found extensive clumps of tubers growing in the moist forest soil and gathered berries that had reached their peak sweetness in this late season of warmth. Fish and meat were drying over smoky fires in preparation for the winter months. The clan did not know how long winter would last in this new world, but Fein reckoned that they should plan on enough dried food to get them through eight moons as they would have in their old homeland. He hoped that winter would not last that long here.

Since they had landed, another baby had been born to one of the women of the clan. Briga named her daughter Anu after their goddess of fertility in hopes that she would be a source of future generations in the Place of Oisin. Briga walked into the forest a few days after Anu's birth to look for berries. Unaware of any threat, Briga held up her leather tunic hem in one hand and dropped the fat blue berries into the fold.

A large, black bear smelled the intoxicating aroma of the smoking meat and came to investigate. The bear crept to within ten feet of Briga, wondering what this strange animal was. The bear raised up behind Briga on its back legs and roared to scare off the obviously much inferior animal. Briga turned and screamed as she saw the black bear towering over her. Her apron-full of berries fell to the ground at her feet. The bear quickly closed the distance and grabbed Briga in its deadly embrace, its claws cutting deeply into her back, and its muzzle biting with a crushing force into her left shoulder.

The clan heard her screams and came running. They found the bear whipping Briga's lifeless body back and forth effortlessly. Several men surrounded the bear and thrust their stone-tipped spears into its body. The bear roared in pain, mortally wounded, and dropped Briga's body to the ground. Two more men hurried in with their spears and killed the bear. Sadly they saw they were too late to save Briga. Her death made it clear to the clan that they had not arrived at the Otherworld; they were still in the mortal world where people were born, grew old and, as so unfortunately revealed, died.

Another nursing mother took over Anu's care. This mother's son could easily do without her milk as he would soon join the other boys nearing the age of initiation into manhood.

Briga's funeral would be of great importance to the clan. Not only would it commemorate those lost at sea and unable to receive a proper burial, but it would symbolize the incorporation of the first spirit of the clan to commune with the other spirits of this new world. Fein hoped that Briga would intercede with the spirits and with Aron, the ruler of the Otherworld, to ensure that his clan received favorable treatment here—wherever here was.

Fein and Briga's husband walked through the forest in search of a proper place for their house of the dead. They found a small stream running through a plateau several hundred feet above the river. They chose this high ground as the most suitable burial place. With the help of the rest of the men in the clan, Fein prepared the spot to receive the first of their dead. They cleared the underbrush from a wide area and brought baskets of soil to create a proper burial mound. They also brought large stones from the shore to surround the grave site.

Once the women had prepared Briga's body, they carried her up to the site chosen for her funeral. Fein's men had dug a shallow grave to receive her body. They lined the grave with aromatic pine bark and placed Briga's body tenderly into the trench. They placed the basket she had brought from the old country at her feet, filled with nuts and berries to sustain her on her journey. Also at her feet, they placed the head of the bear that had killed her. In memory of Oisin, Fein placed a large, ornamental spear point on Briga's stomach. After covering her with more bark strips, they carefully filled the trench with soil and then surrounded it with a ring of smooth, round stones from the river shore. Over the stones they piled soil to create a proper burial mound—one that could always be located and never mistaken for a natural formation.

Fein spoke for the clan, commending Briga's spirit to Aron. He also remembered Oisin and the other clan members who had died in the storm that blew them to this new land. He asked Aron to welcome their spirits to the Otherworld and to look benevolently on the rest of the clan members living in the new land. Then they returned to their campsite for another ceremony—the sacrifice to Manan of a fawn they had captured. As the fawn's blood seeped into the altar they had erected, Fein called on the great sea god to accept the animal in lieu of any more clan members. He asked Manan to welcome Oisin and his spirit companions to the Otherworld and entreated the sea god to ensure that the clan would be safe when they ventured on the water in the future. Fein felt confident they had done all they could to appease the gods.

Anu, daughter of Briga, looked forward to her union with Lug, son of Ogm and grandson of Fein. Having lived thirteen cycles of the seasons, Anu considered herself a woman and ready for the responsibilities within the clan that womanhood entailed. The village dedicated to Oisin had expanded from the original fifty-eight settlers to 160—the sum total of all humans in the new world. Twenty-two of the first women to arrive had given birth to 180 children during the first thirteen cycles of the seasons, Anu being the first of the children born in their new world. Twenty percent of those children had died before maturity. In addition, six women had died in the interim mostly from complications related to childbirth. One old man had died after a long illness during the same period.

The settlement occupied a large area along the cliff above the river shore. Twenty-three shelters provided their dwelling space, situated close together. The rest of the camp site held wooden racks over hearths for drying fish and game, stretchers for working hides of various animals including deer, bear, panther, muskrat, rabbit and beaver, and places for their boats.

Inside their dwellings they had baskets woven from wood strips and from grasses and reeds for storage of food, medicinal herbs, kindling, and the other essentials of life. One corner of their dwellings often held the litter of stone chips, bone and wood fragments that resulted from the making of spear points, knives, scrapers, needles and other tools. The hearth contained the remnants of many meals including animal bones, fish scales, nut hulls, fruit pits and berry seeds.

Anu and her mate would erect their own shelter soon—a ceremonial milestone in which the whole clan would participate. Since Anu soon would give birth and cold weather was approaching, she was eager to get their shelter built. Although the old pioneers who had made the voyage across the sea thought of the dark season in their new land as mild, Anu and the other members of her generation had no way to appreciate that—this world, all they knew, was cold enough for them when the nights grew long. She would make her new home as warm and comfortable as she could for Lug and their child when it came.

All the older clan members were pleasantly amazed at the mildness of the climate. The snows began in earnest at the time when day equaled night, and by the corresponding time six moons later, geese flying overhead, away from the sun, heralded the coming of the fertile soil—the period when the long days warmed the land and it burst in a profusion of growing things. The warm season in the new land grew hotter and lasted longer than Fein's clan was accustomed to, but no one complained.

The rivers still froze solid during the dark time, denying the clan access to the fish and shellfish. Likewise, the coniferous forest provided little to sustain them during the cold season. The clan's diet during the time of long nights consisted of the dried meats and fish they had preserved and a few wild tubers they dug in the forest before the ground froze hard. They were a hardy and resourceful lot, not plagued by much sickness and relatively safe from predators, so survival was not too great a challenge.

They anticipated the coming rebirth of the warm season as the sun wrested control of life away from the moon. Their spiritual leader tracked the passage of time by noting the length of days and the moon phases as marks on a piece of deer pelvis. He knew that the days would grow shorter as the cold weather set in. Three moons after the longest night the climate would be more comfortable and the green of the Earth's renewal would be on the land. The animals that the clan depended on would be more vulnerable at this time of birth and would be more easily caught. The migratory birds would return to the open waterways, providing additional food. Access to the river and the seasonal influx of spawning fish renewed the clan's feelings of hope and good fortune.

They adapted to the lack of natural caves for dwellings by inventing artificial caves built of mounded soil walls, spanned by bent tree boughs covered in an inner layer of woven matting, a middle layer of tree bark, and an outer covering of soil. The inspiration for these dwellings came one day when one of the oarsmen reminded Fein of how well protected they were when they took shelter under their upturned boats. The first shelters looked like upside down boats supported by low earthen walls. Eventually, the designs evolved into broader and longer structures, tall enough for men to walk erect inside. Adequate ventilation allowed them to keep fires burning continually inside their new artificial caves.

These manmade caves didn't provide the security from marauders or wild animals that their caves in the old world afforded, nor were they as well insulated from the cold. However, the clan members soon became comfortable in them since they eventually realized that there were no predators powerful or fierce enough to attack them in a group, and they had encountered no other humans—hostile or friendly.

For weeks, Lug and his friends had been cutting tall saplings about three inches thick at the base for use in constructing Anu's house. Anu and her friends had also been busy weaving long sections of matting made from thin strips of wood peeled from the soft layers beneath the tree bark. Once they had all the materials prepared, Lug went to Fein to formally request permission to erect Anu's house. This ceremony initiated the clan's celebration of the union of Lug and Anu. The whole clan participated in constructing the house. The boys carried the poles to the work site and handed them to the young men who inserted the thickest end into a hole in the ground and then bent the long poles into the bow shape that formed the ribs of the shelter. The poles were placed one arm's length apart and, in the case of Anu's house, their bowed shape spanned a distance of five paces. The skeleton of the dwelling was supported by horizontal poles lashed to each rib along the full length of the house, which was eight paces. Once the bowed framework stood securely, the ends of the structure received vertical poles to partially close them, leaving openings on either end for entrances.

The men of the clan made quick work assembling the framework. The young men showed off their agility walking along the poles high in the air, and the old men offering advice that the young men pretended to ignore. Next, the women brought the mats over and handed them up to the men to secure to the ribs of the house. A small opening was left in the center of the roof to allow the smoke to escape. Finally, the men placed stones around the base of the shelter and added layers of tree bark and soil part way up the sides of the house for insulation against the drafts that could blow under the sides and through the matting. Inside, the men had installed poles across the house for structural support and also to provide a loft area where Anu could store food, clothing and other household items. All that remained for Lug and Anu was to build their sleeping platform inside the shelter and to dig their cooking pit and line it with stones. The latter task fell to Anu and her women friends.

That night, Anu and Lug moved into the newest house in the village. But before they did, the clan held a celebration that included a speech by Fein recognizing the union of Lug and Anu, and followed, too quickly Fein thought, by a feast. He had much more he would have liked to say, but the clan hurried him along, telling him the food would be spoiled by so many long words. Well into the night, after the communal fire had burned down to a warm glow, Lug pulled Anu away from their friends and took her to her new house and to the bed they both had prepared. In the dim light cast by their own hearth, they saw the aromatic bouquet of herbs and flowers left there in secret by one of the clan members.

Anu relished the secure feeling of her first night in her new house as Lug's woman. They lay under the warm skin blanket Anu had stitched as part of her new household goods. Soon Lug fell asleep, tired from the hard work he had done and the feasting. Anu lay awake for a while thinking, as she often did, about the mother she didn't know and her foster mother whom she knew and loved, but ultimately lost to old age. She wished they could have been alive to see this day, but she thought perhaps they could see her from their home in the Otherworld. She hoped so as she drifted off to sleep.

During the warm weather, the men of the village ranged far away, following the river as far as they could in their boats and then trekking on foot up the coastal plain. They searched for seals to be used for food and clothing and to build new boats. They also occasionally encountered mastodon which they killed and butchered on the spot, drying the surplus meat to preserve it and also to make it easier to carry back to the village. They particularly prized the ivory tusks for making tools and ornaments.

While her husband was away hunting, Anu went into labor and gave birth to a boy. The village women helped her through her first and most critical delivery. Her body at thirteen, while sexually mature, had not fully grown, and her narrow pelvic girdle made for a very painful delivery. But she and the baby survived the ordeal. Her subsequent pregnancies and deliveries would be easier as her frame stretched to accommodate the birthing process. The other women also helped with the care of the new baby, each one eager for the opportunity to hold the infant. Anu and Lug had agreed what to name the baby: if a girl, Briga; if a boy, Oisin. In this way they would honor the memory of ones lost in bringing the clan to their new land. Fein beamed with joy at the sight of his great-grandson and cried unashamedly when told the baby's name.

The men of the clan were mystified and suspicious of the entire process of conception, pregnancy and birth. They knew instinctively how conception is caused by intercourse, but only on a broad level of understanding. How a baby formed inside its mother was strictly a magical art controlled exclusively by women. The men believed in some form of spiritual transfer from male to female at the time of impregnation. Thus they believed that part of a man's spirit went into the woman to live and grow inside, eventually emerging as a baby.

The birth of a boy indicated that the mother's spirit did not interfere with the growing process. But the birth of a girl baby was considered by the men as a sign that the mother's spirit had entered and altered the man's spirit while inside the mother and had somehow emasculated the new life. They viewed this with suspicion, alarm and distrust. That was why the men showed little interest in the birth of girl babies. The boys received the interest of the males in the clan as well as the nurturing of the women. The girls remained more isolated with the women.

Anu was proud to have given birth to the spirit of Lug without interfering with it. The baby was strong and healthy and would make Lug and Ghlir as proud as Fein obviously was. Fein had brought all the men of the village around to see his new great-grandson. Many babies had been born into the clan since they reached their new world, but no baby had received so much attention. The child would surely succeed to the leadership of a clan when he matured. Fein bragged that one day Oisin would rule over a number of affiliated clans occupying a large portion of their exciting new world.

Fein's right arm still throbbed with pain. His old injury had made it difficult to do any strenuous work, and Fein soon found himself relegated to the unwelcome role of observer. More and more, his eldest son Ghlir, Lug's father, had taken over the day-to-day decisions for the clan. Fein still enjoyed the respect of the clan, but he and they recognized that soon a new leader would have to take over. Ghlir discussed plans with his father in private before he announced them to the rest of the clan.

Frequently, the actions of the clan now evolved from Ghlir's ideas rather than his father's. Fein knew his time in the mortal world was nearly gone. He would spend his few remaining years as an elder statesman, content to let his son assert his own authority over the clan. The size of the clan had reached the point where a natural interest in subdividing into two clans would occur, and Fein and his son had talked about this eventuality. Ghlir wanted to keep everyone in one village for security but also for personal reasons—to increase his perceived authority. But Fein counseled him on the natural order of these things—the importance of spreading out into the land to avoid conflict over areas of forage and hunting, and the opportunity to develop kin-linked subsidiary clans. Ghlir concluded that he could maintain his authority over the second clan and accepted the inevitable subdivision. Finally, before the onset of cold weather imposed further delay, Ghlir selected three men and sent them out to scout for a suitable location for a new settlement farther down river where the two rivers meet.

The three men Ghlir had sent out to look for a suitable village site returned in seven days with exciting news. They had found an ideal spot for the village on the main river just before it divided into the two branches. There they found high ground overlooking the river with a stream running into the land that made a suitable landing for their boat. They reported that from the vantage point of this site they could draw on the resources of the main river as well as the abundant fish and game on the smaller river branch on which their original village sat. Their chosen site was far enough away to ensure that the two villages did not have to compete for the same fish and game, but close enough that they could easily travel between the two villages by boat in less than one day.

The trip downstream had taken only half of the daylight time due to the strong current that helped propel their boat, but the return trip, against the flow had taken twice as long. Fein and Ghlir listened to the three men describe their expedition, questioning them on what other sites they had considered and why they had been gone so long if the spot they selected was only one day's journey away. Rather than explain the delay, the men took Fein and Ghlir down to their boat, still pulled up on the shore below the steep bank at the edge of the village. When they reached the boat, Fein and Ghlir saw that it contained a huge quantity of fish—some of the largest they had ever seen. One in particular was much longer than the tallest man in the clan.

The scouts explained that the fish swam right up along the shore of their river and they easily speared them from the boat. One of the strongest fish had pulled the boat nearly across the main river before it finally gave up its struggle and allowed the men to pull it into the boat. They were excited by their adventure downriver and by the success of their fishing expedition as well as the site they recommended for the new village.

Fein and Ghlir talked privately in Ghlir's house for a while, and then Ghlir called the whole clan together to announce his decision. Fein stood by him as he addressed the clan. He told them that it was time to start a second settlement for the good of the clan. Everyone in the village had expected this announcement. They wondered who would be selected to go to the new location and also where it would be. Ghlir had the three scouts describe the place they had found. By now, everyone in the village had seen the boatload of fish. Women of the village had begun cooking several of the largest fish to celebrate the return of the three scouts. They had lined a pit with stones heated on the fire and then placed the three fish on top of the stones. After covering them with herbs and slabs of aromatic wood, they covered the wood with a layer of soil to keep the heat from escaping. The rest of the fish had been split, cleaned and placed on drying racks over a smoky fire to preserve them.

Ghlir told the assembled clan members that he had selected thirty-five of them—five family groups—to form the new settlement. They would take two of the large boats and three smaller fishing boats to the new site. He then identified the five men with their women and children who would be separated from the settlement to form the new sub-clan and build the new village downriver. Ghlir and Fein had discussed who should be selected for this new enterprise for several weeks, and they had come to agreement with some difficulty. Ghlir wanted his son Lug to lead the expedition, but Fein could not bear to be separated from Lug, Anu and his new great-grandson, Oisin. Ghlir finally agreed with his father, and selected one of the other men of the clan whom he trusted. Both Ghlir and Fein knew that the ultimate leader of this separate village would have to prove himself to the others just as Fein had done many years before. They hoped that the process would be peaceful. With no competing clans to defend against, the new village should be able to grow harmoniously and the leader's job should not be too challenging.

That evening a celebration and feast helped the members of the clan get over the natural anxiety and sadness of seeing loved ones and close relatives separated into a new settlement. The next day, the thirty-five adventurers had packed their belongings for the short journey to the new site. As they stood by their boats on the shore waiting to depart, the clan's spiritual leader blessed them and called on the river god to make their passage to their new home safe and fruitful. The spiritual leader's acolyte was among the thirty-five. He would see to the spiritual needs of the new settlement, having learned his knowledge of the mystical lore of the clan from his aged mentor. Now that the acolyte was leaving, the spiritual leader would have to begin training someone else to eventually replace him. He was as old as Fein, thirty-eight cycles of the seasons, and his health had begun to fail. He knew he would journey to the Otherworld soon.

The whole clan then said their goodbyes and the members of the new settlement boarded their boats and let the swift current take them out into the channel of the river. Waves from those on shore were reflected by those in the boats and soon the five boats rounded a bend in the river. As the boats disappeared from view, a majestic blue heron rose up from the reeds at the water's edge and soared above the boats, beating its broad wings in a slow, fluid motion that resembled the rhythmic motion of the oars, and, for a few moments, accompanied the new clan on their journey.

With some sadness, the remaining clan members climbed the hill and returned to their customary village duties. Some envied those who had left to build the new village. Others hoped that nothing unpleasant would befall the ones who had left the clan. But soon their thoughts turned to their own lives and daily tasks.

Within one moon, the new village stood on the bank of the wide river as if it had been there for years. They had cleared land within the trees lining the river shore and had constructed six houses. The men and their families occupied five of these houses, and the spiritual leader lived and conducted his incantations in the sixth house. Near the shore of the creek that flowed into the land, they had built their fish and game drying racks, and they had cleared areas to beach their boats. Life had quickly settled into a routine once they had done the hard work of felling trees, cutting saplings for shelter frames and weaving the mats to complete their houses. The men had no difficulty providing their food. In fact, they greatly enjoyed fishing and hunting in their new surroundings far enough removed from the old village that the beasts of the forest had little initial fear of man. The fish had finally migrated away from the river as the cold weather set in, and the men concentrated on taking shellfish from the river and creek, and stalked the deer in the forest.

The new village had stockpiled a large supply of fish and meat to get them through the winter. The women had also stored great quantities of edible roots and tubers they had dug in the forest. As the season of darkness wore on and the meat and fish were used up they would subsist on the remains of the women's foraging for plants. But this village would survive its first cold season easily and would prosper at their pleasant location.

Within a few years the ten young women of the village had increased the size of the community by thirty births. Two thirds of the infants had survived and the village was well on its way to doubling in size within five years. The accumulated debris of life in the village became trodden into the soil; animal bones, shells, nuts, seeds, discarded flint projectiles, and inadvertently lost ornaments became covered with the buildup of soil swept into corners of their shelters and in the common areas of the community. In time the village would be abandoned, and, over the millennia, humus in the forest would decompose into additional layers of soil. Erosion from upland areas would carry even more soil onto the site of this second village, burying it several feet deep. The river beyond the high bank would gradually change from fresh water to salt water, would become influenced by the great tidal surges and would create a new shore at the edge of the village. And new settlers would come to this pleasant spot, yearning for the same access to the beautiful, wide river and its abundant resources.

Fein and Ghlir had devoted themselves to ensuring that the clan would grow and prosper in this new land. After Briga's spirit soared to the Otherworld and the fawn was offered to Manan in memory of Oisin, the gods favored the clan with great prosperity in their new land. Fein and the clan members remembered Briga and Oisin, and they devoutly believed that their intercession with the gods had ensured the clan's safety and prosperity.

Fein's followers knew they had come to some strange new part of the mortal world—not the Otherworld. But the spirits seemed strong in this new land. They found many mystical attributes to the land that they revered, dedicating them to their old world gods. The swift river that ran past their first encampment received regular offerings and prayers to ensure that it would continue to provide the plentiful fish, turtles and muskrats that made up an important part of their diet. The second settlement found similar features of the world that they revered. They also avoided a particular hillock in the forest because they felt it might be a fairy mound where anyone straying too close would be enticed into the Otherworld—never to return.

Briga's daughter, Anu, had produced three children by the time of her sixteenth warm season. Likewise, other women in the clan had recovered quickly from the hardships of their voyage and Fein took pleasure in the sounds of renewal all around him. The oldest pioneer had died, but he had lived longer than anyone would have expected—37 cycles of the seasons. Fein took heart in his companion's longevity and hoped that he would be among his clan as long.

Fein's followers would not know war during his lifetime. Many more generations would succeed before his descendents—grown, divided into many other clans and spread into other parts of their new world—would succumb to the inherently human competitive spirit and make war on their distant kin.

In time, Fein's descendents spread from the Atlantic to the Pacific coast and on the way they met other, more recent visitors from Asia. The clans from various parts of the world fused into the Native American tribes that remained undisturbed by outsiders until the coming—11,000 years later—of more European adventurers in boats similar to Fein's. Their contact with the second wave of Europeans was of little consequence until the 1500s. At that time, aggressive explorers with their weapons and diseases, followed by an unending influx of European colonists, would result in the near total destruction of Fein's descendents and their counterparts from Asia.

Fein's people left little to mark their coming into the new land. The deep, freely flowing river channels began to fill with sediment as they cleared land for their primitive agriculture. In these fertile shallows, the marsh grasses took root and muskrats burrowed into the reed hummocks that began to encroach on the streams. Shore birds and other creatures expanded into these havens. But Europeans who came much later altered the land in fundamental and irrevocable ways, ways that would infuriate the old gods of the natural world. Their new gods, however, seem to approve.

Descendants of these first people in North America spanned the continent during the next few thousand years. They left their stone implements for modern-day archaeologists to find. At one site in Virginia on the Nottoway River, archaeologists have found traces of these earliest people in North America. As in so many finds, serendipity played a part. Harold Connover, a local farmer, found Indian artifacts in a sand deposit. He led Joseph McAvoy and his associates to the spot and, over a period of years in the early 1990s, McAvoy uncovered a layer of Clovis tools. But the big surprise came when he dug deeper into the stratified soil and found more primitive tools dated to approximately 17,000 years ago. Those tools proved to be the earliest human artifacts found in North America. This site, called Cactus Hill, and the unique stone spear point found there, led Dennis Stanford of the Smithsonian Institution to advance an astounding new theory of how North America was first settled. The preceding fictional account of Fein and his band arriving by sea portrays Stanford's theory that the first Americans came from the Iberian Peninsula by boat approximately 18,000 years ago.

Stanford bases his theory on the apparent evolution of the more refined Clovis tool culture from the Solutrean culture of Western Europe. Both cultures worked stone using the same fluting techniques. The American Clovis tools added the innovation of a deeply-fluted, squared-off base.

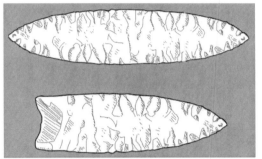

Solutrean Point

Clovis Point

This innovation made the spear points easier to haft into the spear shaft.

Scientists working in DNA analysis have also discovered genetic markers that point to an early infusion of European genes into the earliest American population. Mutations occur in the chromosomes that make up the genetic material of all life on earth including humans. Genetic scientists use mutations of minute portions of chromosomes to trace ancestry in the population. In chromosomes inherited from the maternal line for instance, so-called mitochondrial DNA, genetic scientists have found a pattern designated haplogroup X that is datable to about 20,000 to 30,000 years ago. That is the time when mutations occurred that distinguish this lineage. The emergence of this lineage coincides with the peak of the last Ice Age.

In the Native American population, haplogroup X is one of five haplogroups found. The X-type, however, is not associated with populations from East Asia, whereas the other four haplogroups found in American Indian DNA are of East Asian origin. This implies that the Indian population of North America has ancestors from more than one migratory direction. Clearly, Native Americans are descended from people originating in East Asia, but some also have genetic material brought to America from another region, and that region is apparently modern-day Europe—possibly the Solutrean culture living there at the time of the last Ice Age.

Haplogroup X carrying people could not have come to America over the land bridge from Asia 18,000 to 20,000 years ago. A vast, impenetrable glacier more than one mile thick blocked access to North America for nomads from East Asia until about 13,000 years ago. Haplogroup X occurs in about twenty-five percent of Algonquians, and at a much smaller frequency in other American Indian groups. Stanford and others have concluded that this genetic material, and the characteristic tool technology found at Cactus Hill in Virginia, must have come across the Atlantic Ocean from the Iberian Peninsula.

Even older remains have reportedly been found in the Americas that give evidence of human occupation of the New World as far back as 200,000 years ago. The one site claimed to be this old, Calico Hills in the Mojave Desert east of Los Angeles, was examined briefly by Louis Leakey, famed discoverer of ancient human remains at Olduvai Gorge in Africa.

Leakey found what he believed to be evidence of primitive stone tool construction at Calico Hills. Since his visit, tens of thousands of stones have been collected and presented to the scientific community as evidence of human activity at this site. However, the site remains highly controversial, and the date of the site appears to be much too remote for Homo Sapiens, modern people, to have lived there. Our species of humans evolved in Africa about 200,000 thousand years ago and began migration to other continents about 90 thousand years ago, according to the latest theory. That would make the presence of modern humans in North America 200,000 years ago impossible.

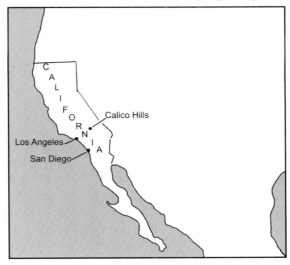

Location of Calico Hills in California

On the other hand, a number of sites in South America could push the date of our species' occupation of the New World back to approximately 30,000 years. Monte Verde in Chile is one such site. Tom Dillehay, an archaeologist working there, found indisputable evidence of humans living there 13,000 years ago. The evidence included a human footprint, wooden timbers, sharpened pegs, cordage made from plant fibers, and remains of foodstuffs including preserved mastodon meat. At a nearby site, he found remains that appear to be much older. This site, at a deeper stratum, yielded stone tools that date to 33,000 years ago.

Monte Verde and Pedra Furada Archaeological Sites

In Brazil at a cave called Pedra Furada, Niède Guidon found a cooking hearth with evidence of stone tool making nearby. Pedra Furada is a rock shelter in which humans lived over a period of thousands of years. Charcoal from the hearth yielded a radiocarbon date indicating people lived there 32,000 years ago. Some scientists dispute the claimed antiquity of Monte Verde and Pedra Furada artifacts, but further analysis may confirm the accuracy of the 30,000 plus years date. Should that happen, we will need to come up with a new theory of who the first people in the Americas were.

Chapter 2
13,000 Years Ago

The great glacier that had completely covered the northern two-thirds of North America had receded significantly in the five thousand years since the world had begun to warm. Although an ice field still bordered the western sea, hundreds of miles inland, an ice-free corridor had opened up freeing an expanse of tundra on which herds of mammoth, elk, and other grazing animals lived.

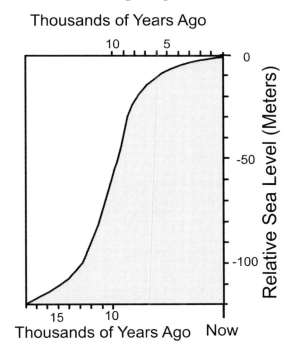

Sea levels had risen about fifty feet since the glaciers had begun to melt, but the bridge between Asia and North America still remained well above sea level. The so-called bridge was in reality a broad expanse of grassland steppe nearly 1,000 miles wide. A population of a few thousand Paleo-Asian nomads had followed migratory animals along that vast neck of land from modern-day Siberia and had become isolated there during the last Ice Age.

These hunter-gatherers, pinned between two impassable glaciers, lived in the land called Beringia. They remained on the grasslands of Beringia from the time the Solutrean people began their crossing of the Atlantic until the North American glacier had melted sufficiently for a corridor to permit their passage south into the heart of the continent, along the eastern slopes of the Rocky Mountains. The Paleo-Asian people were unable to proceed into the new-world continent for 5,000 years. By that time, the earlier Solutrean migrants from Europe had expanded across the breadth of North America, and their stone tool technology had gradually developed into the more refined Clovis spear points.

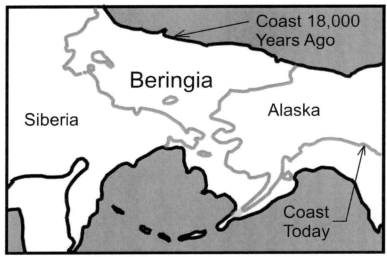

The Bering Land Bridge Between Asia and North America

Even today, the distance from Cape Dezhnev on the Siberian mainland to Wales, Alaska, is little more than fifty miles. Along their route through Beringia, these nomads encountered two mountain peaks towering about 1,300 feet above the sea mid-way between Asia and North America. They followed the prey animals around the base of the mountains—now the twin islands of Big and Little Diomede—on their way to the New World. Then, the migratory animals led them eastward to a vast new land: America.

These newcomers to North America followed the migratory animals through the tundra of modern-day Alaska and Canada along the east side of the Rocky Mountains, then south through a semi-desert region before reaching lush grasslands bordered by boreal forestland. These Asian nomads would meet and interact with other occupants of the New World descended from the earlier Solutrean immigrants. The nature of those contacts cannot be known, but we can assume that some groups merged or at least exchanged members of their clans, while other meetings may have been marked by hostility and combat over issues of territory.

The Paleo-Asian population arriving around 13,000 years ago brought with them their different genetic makeup and also a different tool technology. They specialized in making spears, harpoons, and knives by applying microblades (single stone flakes) to shafts and handles rather than painstakingly flaking larger stones on both faces into the intricately flaked tools characteristic of the Solutrean and Clovis cultures.

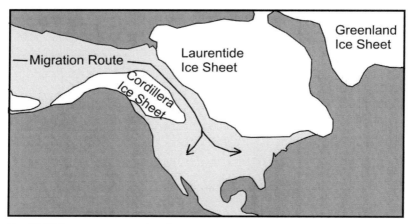

By 13,000 years ago, an ice-free corridor opened as the glacier melted

By 10,000 years ago, the Bering land bridge was breached by the rising sea and Asia was cut off from North America to overland migration from that time onward. So, after several thousand years of possible migration into or out of the arctic region of North America, the avenue was closed and any new migrations from Asia would employ some form of watercraft.

The Asian immigrants brought an entirely different language, with a different culture and belief system. The Solutrean culture in Western Europe would be replaced by the Celtic culture. The culture in Northeast Asia would evolve into the forerunners of the Siberian peoples with their rich mythology and languages that share some characteristics with Native American languages.

During the time of contact in North America between the two disparate cultures (Paleo-Asian and Solutrean) the environment began a rapid transformation. At first, these Paleo-Indians lived in small clan-based groups, held together by kinship. Individuals in the group had to be competent in many skills. They were nomadic hunter-gatherers who followed their prey animals and did not build permanent settlements. As the temperature and sea-level rose, the Native American population responded to those changes in their habitat and in the animal and plant resources available to them.

Ten thousand years ago represents the time of transition from Paleo-Indian culture to what anthropologists call the Archaic culture. During the Archaic period, American Indians began to settle into larger, more stable groups. Their tool kits became more complex; they had invented the spear thrower but not the bow and arrow. They lived in larger groups now, linked by social or political bonds, and they built semi-permanent settlements where they began to depend on wild plants—the forerunner of agriculture.

By 3,000 years ago, the Native American population had progressed further, having developed agriculture, mastered pottery, and improved on their weaponry. The period from 3,000 years ago to the fifteenth century is called Woodland by anthropologists. The earliest contact by the foreign cultures we will examine further in this book occurred during the late Archaic and the Woodland periods.

During the Woodland period, American Indians had developed the complex social, religious, and technological aspects that would be observed and recorded during historic times by the Norse, the Portuguese, the Spanish, the French and finally the English explorers of North America. During the Woodland period, the environment had undergone the greatest changes since the glaciers had begun to melt.

American Indians had developed their agriculture based on the "three sisters" of maize, beans, and squash.

They had capable watercraft, pottery, and complex religious beliefs—that paralleled in many ways the beliefs of Christianity—and they had evolved into many language groups such as Algonquian, Siouan, Iroquoian, Mayan, etc. Each of these groups included numerous tribes with territories throughout the continent. Population density had grown significantly, leading to trade and competition. Conflict developed between tribes of the various language groups. The Native Americans were, for the most part, settled into fiercely held territories controlled by a hierarchy of tribal leaders.

Indian technology was well-adapted to their environment

With this background, we now turn our attention to subsequent voyages to North America by various Old World cultures. Each of these contacts has left some mark on the American landscape, has a documented history, exists in the tradition of the Native Americans, or can be found in the literature of foreign cultures. Prolonged contact with some of these foreign visitors may also have influenced changes in Native American culture and left genetic traces in the native population.

Chapter 3
Red Paint People

In coastal Europe, including Scandinavia and Brittany, seven to eight thousand years ago, a maritime culture had developed to the point that they traveled the sea fishing for deep-sea species and trading goods along the coasts of Europe. There is evidence that their trade network extended as far as the Mediterranean Sea. The oldest megaliths—standing stones—in Europe date to this period.

By four to five thousand years BCE this culture had developed their maritime skills sufficiently to permit them to follow the open seaways across the North Atlantic to the northeast coast of North America. One hallmark of this culture was their use of red ochre (hydrated iron oxide, a naturally occurring mineral). Burials examined dating to seven thousand years ago in Scandinavia and North America show skeletal remains and grave goods coated with this red mineral.

Actually the use of red ochre in burial rituals is not unique to this culture—even some Neanderthal graves contained red ochre. However, the extensive use of red ochre led to the discovery in 1882 of a burial site in Maine when a farmer thought blood was flowing out of a furrow left by his plow. Examination of the site revealed a collection of stone tools that appeared different from the usual Algonquian artifacts found in this region along the Penobscot River. By the beginning of the twentieth century, numerous other Red Paint burial sites had been found in New England and then in Canada.

Modern-day archaeologists have determined that similar sites exist over a wide expanse of coastal New England and Canada, and essentially identical sites have been found in Scandinavia and Brittany dating to the same period. Many more sites probably exist offshore—the sea level has risen about twelve meters (about forty feet) since this culture began, flooding some of their shore-side settlements.

The Red Paint People made their living hunting and fishing, and their bone and stone tools have survived in shell middens in New England and Canada. In addition to the similarity of the tools found in Scandinavia and North America, the remains of dwellings found on both sides of the Atlantic are similar.

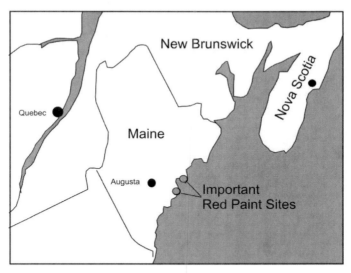

Archaeological sites of Red Paint People in Maine

The Red Paint culture on both sides of the Atlantic left many equivalent artifacts including polished slate gouges used for woodworking, effigies of sea birds, killer whales, and other animals. The simultaneous replacement of flint tools with polished slate tools on both sides of the Atlantic provides the most intriguing coincidence that argues for the contact between people in North America with people in Scandinavia four to five thousand years ago.

Similar geometric design provides another aspect of the artifacts found on both sides of the Atlantic in Red Paint contexts. At both locations, stone tools decorated with a series of lines and dots indicate yet another cultural feature common to these contemporaneous cultures.

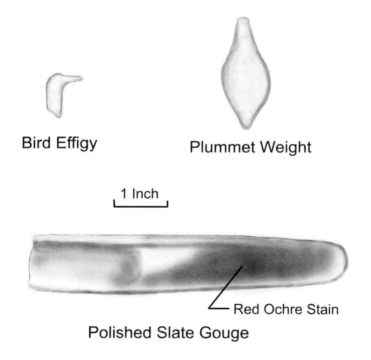

Bird Effigy   Plummet Weight

1 Inch

Red Ochre Stain

Polished Slate Gouge

Typical Red Paint Culture artifacts found in Europe and America

46

Anthropologists fall into two camps with the issue of peopling America: diffusionists and isolationists (aka. independent inventionists). The diffusionists see the Red Paint cultures on both sides of the Atlantic as evidence of contact between people from Scandinavia and native peoples of America. The only stumbling block for these diffusionists is the idea that any people seven or eight thousand years ago had the maritime technology to cross the Atlantic.

This diffusionist/isolationist debate pertains in other parts of the world and at other cultural periods. However, the debate between these two factions of anthropologists regarding the Red Paint People focuses on the principal issue of marine technology. If both factions accepted that people in the sixth millennium BCE could travel across the Atlantic, the debate would not exist. The disbelief among some anthropologists that humans had ocean-going maritime capability that far back leads to elaborate theories to explain how two presumed isolated cultures could develop so many similar characteristics at essentially the same time yet be separated by thousands of miles of ocean.

Isolationists see the many similarities in the Red Paint People in Europe and America as mere coincidences. They argue that the simultaneous development of polished slate tools, the use of similar geometric designs, the carving of the various animal effigy figures, the extensive use of red ochre, all merely represent the tendency of people to innovate equivalent solutions to common problems. This same intellectual sleight of hand dismisses the similarity of pyramids in the Old World and the New World, the similarity of Asian and Mayan iconography and design elements, and other striking aspects suggesting possible contact between Old World and New World cultures as simply coincidence.

As to the argument that people eight thousand years ago did not have the maritime capability to travel the North Atlantic from one continent to the other, that idea becomes hard to defend when we look at the seagoing ability evident in some of the artifacts found in Red Paint sites on both sides of the Atlantic. Bones from fish that can only be caught at great depth at sea—such as the swordfish—occur in these sites. The size of their fishing weights also imply that they had the capability to sail well out to sea to fish in depths of hundreds of feet.

Drawing of a rock carving depicting a boat at Brandskog, Sweden

Remains of boats dating back to the Red Paint period have turned up in archaeological digs in England and on the continent. The oldest boats may have been the type of hide-covered frames described in the first chapter—a type that has continued in use through perhaps twenty thousand years to the modern coracle of the Irish. At some point in the dim past, hide covering was replaced by the plank-covered frame construction of the typical Norse vessels. Rock carvings dating to 2000 BCE depict these sorts of ships.

Whether people from Scandinavia brought the Red Paint culture to America in hide-covered boats or wooden-hulled ships seems a rather fine distinction. The similarity in the Red Paint People on both sides of the Atlantic stems from contact between those previously isolated peoples.

Chapter 4
Fu Sang

Chinese documents contain accounts of voyages to a land far to the east that they called Fu Sang during the reign of their Emperor Shun. Shun reigned about 4,200 years ago, and Chinese history records that he sent astronomers out to make celestial measurements that could be used to develop a map of the known world. By taking these measurements of the stars and planets at remote locations, they could calculate the distance from those locations to their home in China.

Emperor Shun

Those Chinese scholars who traveled to the land of Fu Sang returned with data that allowed them to produce an accurate geography of a land now believed by some to be North America. From their data, a curiously circular map was produced as part of the Shan Hai Jing—reputed to be the oldest known geography. The name translates to "Book of Mountains and Seas." That geography was originally contained in thirty-two books and was later reduced to eighteen. Later commentaries in China testify to the existence and antiquity of this geography. Confucius, who lived 551 to 479 BCE, possessed a copy of the Shan Hai Jing.

A third century BCE writer in China referred to Fu Sang as lying at the eastern perimeter of the ocean we call the Pacific. This writer indicated that the breadth of Fu Sang was 10,000 li (the li being a Chinese measurement of distance equal to about one-third of a mile). That writer also described huge coniferous trees that, in America, could only have been the Giant Sequoia of the Pacific Northwest.

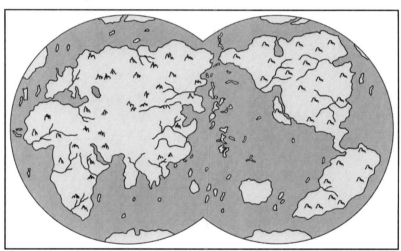

**Drawing based on a Chinese map purported to date to 1418
Note the remarkably accurate depiction of North America**

Many other accounts of Fu Sang, including histories and poems, describe other aspects of the country that fit with North America. According to one translation of the Shan Hai Jing, the geography mentions four surveys of North America from Canada to Mexico that took place about 2200 BCE.

These surveys apparently discovered the Grand Canyon, Baja California, and the high plateau of present-day Mexico City, as well as other notable continental features.

Researcher Henrietta Mertz has compared the account of the surveyors of Fu Sang to modern-day maps and has shown that their descriptions accurately describe: the Pacific Northwest; a slice through the middle of the continent from Montana through Colorado; and the geography of New Mexico and Mexico. These ancient Chinese records identify features such as rivers, mountain peaks, and Native American cultural aspects with clarity and accuracy to within a few miles over a span of thousands of miles. Mertz pointed out that the details extended to the direction of river flows, presence of mineral deposits, style of houses—such as the round houses of the Southwest Indians of that period—and physical descriptions of Native Americans that correspond to our current understanding of those indigenous people of 4,200 years ago. The description of the Grand Canyon conclusively ties the 4,200 year old account of Fu Sang to North America.

Some scholars who have studied the Shan Hai Jing and related antique circular maps now believe that the surveys conducted by the Chinese 4,200 years ago actually took place. They also postulate that the Chinese left people in America to colonize the vast country. Unfortunately, no maps positively dating that far back have been discovered. The maps that do exist and the written geographical accounts, however, do extend well beyond 2,000 years into the past. It seems clear that the Chinese historical record unequivocally claims that Chinese explorers visited America during Shun's reign, and it is equally clear that Chinese maps had more accurate depictions of America long before western maps showed the New World in naïve detail or as "Terra Incognita."

Leaving behind this intriguing but not easily documented account of early Chinese expeditions to America we come to an account that appears to have a better provenance: the voyage of Hui Shan (or Hui Shen, or Hoei Shin), a Buddhist monk who, along with four other monks, sailed to Fu Sang in the year 458 CE. The monks sailed along the coast of China, Korea, Siberia, past the Aleutian Island chain to Alaska, propelled by the Kamchatka current, and then continued down the Pacific coast of North America to California. After an inland sojourn 350 miles to the east, they continued on their journey to Mexico. The account of Hui Shan's voyage was written in a preliminary form soon after he reported to Emperor Wu of the Liang dynasty on his return to China. The formal account of Hui Shan's report contained in the history of the Liang dynasty, printed 130 years after Hui Shan sailed to Fu Sang, has gained acceptance by historians studying the possibility of contact between North America and China in ancient times.

One such scholar, Joseph Needham, while traveling in Mexico, noted the many similarities between the Amerindian and Chinese cultures. He cited the similarity in motifs such as sky-dragons, double-headed serpents, drums, compass symbols, calendars, and paintings. Perhaps most persuasive was the fixation the ancient Chinese, Aztec and Maya had on jade. In all three cultures, examination of grave goods revealed that corpses were buried with jade objects in their mouths and these objects were coated in cinnabar. Many other similarities have been found by scholars knowledgeable of the ancient Chinese and the Native Americans of the first millennium of the Common Era. Needham wrote, "…a mountain of evidence is now accumulating that between the seventh century BC and the sixteenth century AD, that is throughout the pre-Columbian ages, occasional visits of Asian peoples to the Americas took place."

According to an analysis of Hui Shan's report performed by Henrietta Mertz, the Buddhist monks made landfall in California near Point Hueneme, midway between modern-day Los Angeles and Santa Barbara. From there, they traveled 350 miles east, putting them near the modern-day town of Aguila, Arizona. At that location, they encountered the Mogollon people. They described how the society was a matrilineal one; that the men belonged to the Snake Clan, and the women carried their babies in papooses on their back. To the north they found a black gorge—Black Canyon of the Gunnison—and to the south, near the Gulf of California, they observed a smoking volcano, perhaps Volcan de Colima, although there are a number of other candidates in Mexico.

The Buddhists spent most of their time in Mexico, living among the forerunners of the Aztecs in the Valley of Mexico and then spending time among the Maya of Yucatan before returning to the west coast of Mexico. There, they sailed away, returning to China after many years on their journey. The voyage was about 13,000 miles each way. The sailing time alone would have taken them nearly one year. Their explorations of the American Southwest and Mexico must have added several years to their time in Fu Sang.

Henrietta Mertz has examined Mexican legends (Aztec and Mayan) looking for a tie-in to the story of Hui Shan. She has concluded that Hui Shan was the prototype from which the legends of Quetzalcoatl and Kukulcan developed. Those legendary figures, deified by their respective cultures, supposedly brought technology to the Indians of Mexico. Quetzalcoatl and Kukulcan were described as fair complexioned, bearded figures, with peaceful demeanors essentially following the route into and through Mexico taken by Hui Shan.

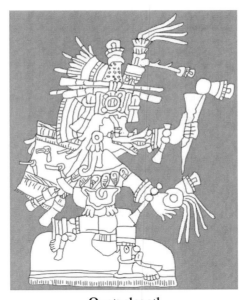

Quetzalcoatl

This legendary figure taught a new religion to the Indians. In their legends, this god sailed away with a promise to return in the year named for him—Ce Acatal in the Nahuatl language. Hernán Cortés, the Spanish conqueror of Mexico happened to arrive in 1519, a year that corresponded to Ce

55

Acatal in the Aztec calendar. Thus, the guardians of the legend of the bearded, holy visitor, Hui Shan/Quetzalcoatl, mistook that bearded conquistador for the Buddhist monk of more than 1,000 years earlier. The mistake had disastrous consequences for the Aztecs.

Hui Shan reported to the Chinese emperor that the people of Fu Sang grew a plant resembling bamboo, which produced pear-shaped fruit bearing kernels—maize. He described their complex calendar, sophisticated architecture, written language, and other signs of technological accomplishment. But in the legend, the bearded holy man evolved into a complex, and at times bloodthirsty god, the giver of all technology including agriculture, writing, and calendars to the Indians of Mexico.

The Hopi of the American Southwest have a parallel legend of the Pahana, their long-lost white brother. Like Quetzalcoatl in Mexico, Pahana was expected to return to the American Southwest to restore peace and harmony among the people there. Pahana could also be a cultural echo of the long ago Buddhist visitor, Hui Shan, who visited their ancestors, the Mogollon people in the fifth century. Pahana would be known when he returned by having in his possession a fragment of a sacred stone tablet given to him before his departure. The Hopi claim that the rest of that stone tablet still exists in their possession awaiting the arrival of Pahana with the missing fragment.

Whether Hui Shan returned to China with a fragment of the stone tablet is not known, but Mertz has interpreted his report to the Chinese emperor as containing a clear description of the Kachina elements of the Mogollon culture.

She concluded that Hui Shan's reference to the men having heads of dogs was indicative of the iconic masks (carved to resemble dogs and other animals) used in the Kachina tradition. Likewise, the Buddhist's report that the native women took snakes as husbands referred to the fact that some of the men belonged to the snake clan. As Hui Shan's report became transcribed and shortened, no doubt the original meaning of what he reported became greatly distorted.

Consequently, the existence of the report of Hui Shan's voyage to North America and his travels among the Indians of the fifth century, coupled with oral traditions in the American Southwest and written history among the Indians of Mexico, referring to the coming of the holy, bearded stranger in their distant past, gives credibility to the theory of contact between China and North America 1,500 years ago if not 4,200 years ago. Needham's statement that "…occasional visits of Asian peoples to the Americas took place" seems justified.

Chapter 5
Phoenician-Israelite Joint Venture

*And King Solomon made a navy of ships in Eziongeber,
which is beside Eloth, on the shore of the Red Sea, in the land
of Edom. And Hiram sent in the navy his servants, shipmen
that had knowledge of the sea, with the servants of Solomon.
And they came to Ophir, and fetched from thence gold, four
hundred and twenty talents, and brought it to King Solomon.* 1
Kings 9:26-28.

*And the navy also of Hiram, that brought gold from
Ophir, brought in from Ophir great plenty of almug trees and
precious stones. For the king had at sea a navy of Tharshish
with the navy of Hiram: once in three years came the navy of
Tharshish, bringing gold, and silver, ivory, and apes, and
peacocks.* 1 Kings 10: 11 and 22.

*And Hiram sent him by the hands of his servants ships,
and servants that had knowledge of the sea; and they went with
the servants of Solomon to Ophir, and took thence four hundred
and fifty talents of gold, and brought them to King Solomon.* 2
Chronicles 8:18.

*For the king's ships went to Tharshish with the servants of
Hiram: every three years once came the ships of Tharshish
bringing gold, and silver, ivory, and apes, and peacocks."* 2
Chronicles 9:21.

These biblical passages give the only documented
evidence we have of King Solomon engaging in naval
expeditions. The following passages from the Hebrew Bible,
the Tanakh, provide essentially the same story.

And King Solomon made a navy of ships in Ezion-geber, which is beside Eloth, on the shore of the Red Sea, in the land of Edom. 1 Kings 9:26.

And Hiram sent in the navy his servants, shipmen that had knowledge of the sea, with the servants of Solomon. 1 Kings 9:27.

And they came to Ophir, and fetched from thence gold, four hundred and twenty talents, and brought it to King Solomon. 1 Kings 9:28.

And the navy also of Hiram, that brought gold from Ophir, brought in from Ophir great plenty of sandal-wood and precious stones. 1 Kings 10:11.

For the king had at sea a navy of Tharshish with the navy of Hiram; once every three years came the navy of Tharshish, bringing gold, and silver, ivory, and apes, and peacocks. 1 Kings 10:22.

Then went Solomon to Eziongeber, and to Eloth, on the sea-shore in the land of Edom. 2 Chronicles 8: 17.

And Hiram sent him by the hands of his servants ships, and servants that had knowledge of the sea; and they came with the servants of Solomon to Ophir, and fetched from thence four hundred and fifty talents of gold, and brought them to king Solomon. 2 Chronicles 8: 18.

You might wonder what these obscure biblical passages have to do with our story of the peopling of America. There is a clue in the American Southwest that mariners during the time of King Solomon may have visited the New World and left a record of their visit there.

King Solomon on his throne

Historians and biblical scholars have never satisfactorily determined where the land of Ophir was. From the biblical accounts we know that King Solomon and Hiram, who was King of Tyre, formed an alliance that made Hiram's experienced seamen available to Solomon for a joint trading enterprise. They sailed on ships commissioned by Solomon to Ophir, returning in three years with great treasures of gold, silver, precious stones, ivory, apes, sandalwood, and peacocks. The biblical text seems to imply that the ships were based at Tharshish.

A Phoenician city of that name sat at the mouth of the modern-day Guadalquivir River in Spain. That river flows into the Gulf of Cadiz near modern-day Jerez de la Frontera. However, some scholars assert that the biblical reference to ships of Tharshish merely refers to a type of ship rather than the point of departure of the ships on the voyage to Ophir. Still others identify Tharshish with Carthage and other locations. So we cannot positively identify the point of origin of the joint expeditions of Phoenician and Israelite traders.

Drawing of Phoenician ship taken from bas relief on a sarcophagus

Tyre was a powerful city of Phoenicia in Canaan (now Lebanon) at the time of Solomon's reign. Hiram ruled Tyre during its golden age. His navy traded in North Africa, and eventually Phoenician vessels ventured through the Straits of Gibraltar into the Atlantic Ocean. One indication of Phoenician expansion is that people as far away as modern-day Portugal worshipped the Phoenician deities, Baal and Astarte. The Phoenicians founded the city of Gades—modern-day Cadiz in Spain—in 1,110 BCE, about the time of King Solomon.

One of the Phoenicians' exports, purple dye extracted from the murex shell, was prized in all the Mediterranean kingdoms, and the Greek word for blood-red—*phoinos*—is the origin of the name Phoenicians.

They imported tin from modern-day Britain for use in making bronze. By 450 BCE, Hanno of Carthage, a Phoenician, had sailed as far south along the African Atlantic coast as Guinea. They may also have circumnavigated Africa on a voyage that departed the Red Sea under sponsorship of an Egyptian pharaoh as early as 600 BCE.

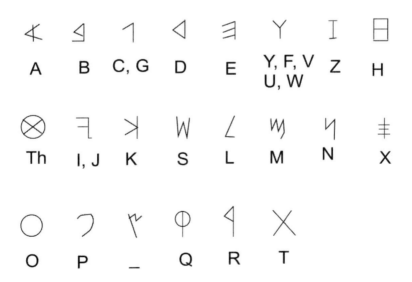

Phoenician Alphabet

Phoenicians made extensive use of writing and shared their alphabet (a precursor to the modern alphabet) with the Israelites of the first millennium BCE. They spoke a language of the Semitic group that also included the language of the Israelites. The close cooperation between Hiram and Solomon included not only the joint maritime trading expeditions but also the building of the first great temple in Jerusalem.

Back to the American Southwest: near the small town of Los Luñas, about twenty miles south of Albuquerque, New Mexico, stands Mystery Mountain. Ancient petroglyphs and rock paintings exist all over the Southwest. The Albuquerque area is no exception. Most petroglyphs depict sun discs, snakes, birds, ducks, stick figures of people, or geometric designs. Native Americans produced those artworks and American Indians acknowledged them as the work of their ancestors when questioned by early European explorers and later American settlers who pushed west after American independence.

Typical Indian petroglyphs of the Southwest

However, on Mystery Mountain there is one petroglyph that the Indians do not take credit for and are as mystified about as the non-Indians who have studied it. American settlers first saw this petroglyph in 1800. The petroglyph appeared to be some unknown form of writing inscribed on a volcanic boulder at the base of the mountain. On an area of the boulder about four feet by two feet, the following inscription appears:

I am Jehovah, the eternal Eloah, your god, who brought you out of the land of Mitsrayim, out of the house of bondage. You shall not have other gods in place of me. You shall not make for yourself molded idols. You shall not lift up your voice to connect the name of Jehovah in hate. Remember you the Sabbath to make it holy. Honor your father and your mother to make long your existence upon the land which Jehovah Eloah gave to you. You shall not murder. You shall not commit adultery. You shall not steal. You shall not bear witness against your neighbor, testimony for a bribe. You shall not covet the wife of your neighbor and all which belongs to your neighbor.

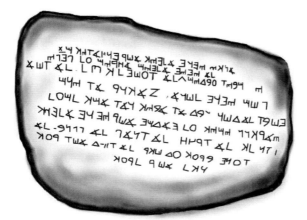

The Los Luñas Rock

This inscription is, of course, not carved in English, nor in any modern language; the inscription is in an ancient Semitic script with a few Greek letters and some anomalous characters inserted. Although linguistic scholars have advanced a number of theories on how old the inscription is, ranging from 3,000 to 1,500 years, other evidence seems to argue for the older date.

In the 1980s, geologist George Morehouse examined the rock, the carved inscriptions, and the natural patina on the surface of the stone. He estimated that the carving was anywhere from five hundred to thousands of years old. Further, the rock has settled, tilting to an angle of forty degrees since it was inscribed—another indication of antiquity.

The late Frank Hibbins, a New Mexico Archaeologist, examined the inscription in 1933. At that time, he said he found it covered with lichen and the carved letters were hardly visible. Hibbins said the elderly man who led him to the inscription claimed to have first seen it in the 1880s. The Semitic language of the inscription was not translated until the twentieth century, making it unlikely that a hoaxer had carved the inscription prior to its discovery by Hibbins guide.

Unfortunately, Hibbins' association with the Los Luñas artifact causes some problems. Hibbins led archaeological excavations in the Southwest in the 1930s. After service as an aide to the Joint Chiefs of Staff, he resumed his pursuit of archaeology. Later examination of some of his work revealed that Hibbins was inaccurate at best and sometimes misrepresented his data to advance his theories of the antiquity of humans in America. He may even have reported finding a site of early man in Alaska that "never existed" according to archaeologist James Dixon of the University of Colorado. Although there is no evidence that Hibbins made the inscription on the Los Luñas rock, it cannot be ruled out. On the other hand, Hibbins made no great claim for the antiquity of the Los Luñas inscription. In the 1930s, he estimated that the inscription was at least one hundred years old based on the growth of lichens and moss covering the inscription. Had he wished to offer the artifact as evidence of travelers from the time of King Solomon, he surely would have asserted that the inscription was much older than one hundred years.

The text seems to be genuine; the roughly eighty-ton boulder was not a souvenir found in the Middle-East and transported to New Mexico. The only non-Native American people known to have been in this area before the 1800s were sixteenth-century Spanish explorers. They would not have had the capability to write the Ten Commandments in ancient Semitic script, nor would they have had any logical reason to do so. On the other hand, Spaniards left numerous inscriptions in their language and western alphabet in the Southwest region of America.

Accepting that the inscription is genuine, and perhaps of the period of King Solomon, that leaves the question: who carved the inscription? There seem to be two possibilities. One of King Solomon's "servants" could have carved the inscription or it could have been one of King Hiram's "shipmen," since they sailed together. The religious nature of the inscription points to one of the Israelites rather than a

Phoenician who would have worshipped Baal, Astarte, or any of their other gods.

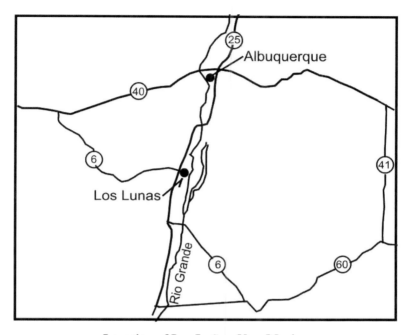

Location of Los Luñas, New Mexico

Ophir must have been a distant and exotic land to the people of the Mediterranean. There is no way of knowing how many Phoenician-Israelite voyages came from the Mediterranean Sea or Iberia to America; nor do we know if any of the men remained in America. However, seamen sometimes remained behind in other areas at other times due to willful abandonment of the expedition or abandonment by the expedition leaders. Thus it seems possible that one or more of the members of the expedition dispatched by King Solomon could have remained among the Native Americans when his ship returned to the Mediterranean or Red Sea.

The site of this enigmatic inscribed rock is located very near the Puerco River, a tributary of the Rio Grande. Phoenician ships or smaller craft could have navigated from the mouth of the Rio Grande to this general area. There they probably would have encountered the ancestors of the Pueblo Indians living in that area today such as the Acoma people. Unlike the legends of Central America and Arizona concerning the bearded holy man—Hui Shan/Quetzalcoatl/Pahana—there appears to be no mythological cultural memory of the Phoenicians or Israelites visiting New Mexico 3,000 years ago. Perhaps they had little impact on the Native Americans, or it may be that the passage of 3,000 years has erased the memory from the tribal consciousness of the Indians inhabiting the American Southwest today.

We cannot say that America was the Ophir referred to in the Bible. In fact some Biblical scholars put Ophir east of modern-day Israel, perhaps at a location on the Red Sea. Some think Ophir may have referred to India. Ophir remains a point of scholarly debate and no one has conclusively identified its location, but the inscription of the Ten Commandments on that boulder at Mystery Mountain makes it possible that someone of the time of Solomon or from a period as recent as 1,500 years ago visited modern-day New Mexico. That person knew the ancient Semitic alphabet and the dialect of the early Biblical time as well as an ancient version of the Ten Commandments. If genuine, the Los Luñas rock indicates contact between the Old World and the New World a millennium at least before Christopher Columbus's expeditions to America.

Chapter 6
Woden-lithi, Tadach, & Iaguntxo

Even before the time that King Solomon's explorers might have reached modern-day New Mexico, Woden-lithi, King of Ringerlike in Norway, may have left a rock-carved message in Ontario, Canada, in 1700 BCE, saying that he had sailed in his ship *Gungnir* there to trade for copper ingots with the local inhabitants—Algonquian Indians. He was there five months and then sailed back to Norway. Woden-lithi's inscriptions can be seen on the face of a rocky outcrop near Peterborough in what is now a Canadian national park site.

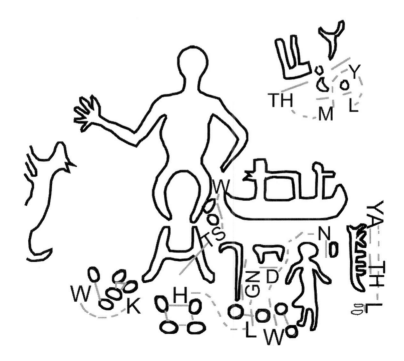

A portion of the petroglyphs at Peterborough, Ontario, Canada
Modern letters have been written next to the equivalent ancient letters

The preceding sketch of part of the Peterborough inscriptions provides the following text (lacking vowels): WK HLGN TSIW WDN LTHY. With the addition of vowels, the inscription reads: "Wilk halgen Tsiwa Woden-Lithi," or "This image hallowed to Tsiwa (a Norse God) by Woden-Lithi."

According to the late Professor Barry Fell, the complete inscription (much of which is not shown in the sketch) yields this record of Woden-lithi's visit to anyone conversant in the Tifinag, Ogham, and phonoglyphs that Woden-lithi used to inscribe his message.

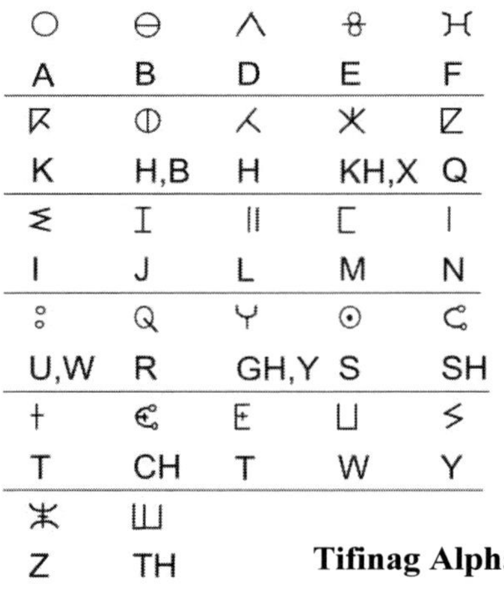
A B D E F
K H,B H KH,X Q
I J L M N
U,W R GH,Y S SH
T CH T W Y
Z TH

Tifinag Alphabet

In other words, unless you are a specialist in epigraphy, you will not even see that there is a message carved in this rock wall. And there's the problem. For most of the time that modern-day archaeologists have known about this site, they have referred to the carvings as Native American petroglyphs. Untrained in epigraphy, archaeologists have not recognized that the site contains a message from Norse traders dating back nearly four thousand years. Many archaeologists and even some experts in the ancient languages and alphabets dispute Professor Fell's translation of this message.

However, at least one renowned expert in these languages, Professor David Kelley, the man who deciphered Mayan glyphs, supports much of what Professor Fell has found in America regarding ancient visits recorded in various locales, including his translation of the message at Peterborough. Kelley said, "Despite my occasional harsh criticism of Fell's treatment of individual inscriptions, it should be recognized that without Fell's work there would be no [North American] Ogham problem to perplex us. We need to ask not only what Fell has done wrong in his epigraphy, but also where we have gone wrong as archaeologists in not recognizing **such an extensive European presence in the New World**." (Emphasis added). Kelley also said, "It looks to me as if a single trade route united an area from the gold-mining zone along the Niger to Scandinavia, and I think that oceanic voyagers from Scandinavia, linked into that route, reached Ontario."

Beyond the evidence of the petroglyphs, an incredible amount of copper is missing from the ancient mines along the north shore of Lake Superior and Isle Royale. Radiocarbon dating of charcoal in the roughly 5,000 mining sites there revealed that Native American people extracted copper from these mines between three and four thousand years ago, and Susan R. Martin, writing in *The Michigan Archaeologist,* asserted that Native Americans might have been mining copper as much as seven thousand years ago.

Perhaps fifty million pounds of copper (not copper ore but pure copper metal) were taken from these mines. That far exceeds the amount of copper believed to have existed within the Native American domestic sites. Michigan contains large outcrops of essentially pure copper, some of which has been found on the surface, while more exists in extensive underground seams easily accessible to ancient miners. Some people believe that the bulk of that Lake Superior copper mined thousands of years ago made its way to Europe and the Mediterranean to be forged along with tin from Cornwall into various Bronze-Age (3,300 to 1,200 BCE) items.

Undoubtedly, some of what Fell has written about will be rejected in time by solid, scholarly review. However, so many discoveries showing not only European but Mediterranean and African contact with Native Americans dating back thousands of years cannot be dismissed as random scratches made by farmers' plows, Colonial era root cellars, or merely coincidental similarities to Old World designs and motifs— the arguments offered so far by archaeologists. In this chapter, we will look at a few more of the compelling finds that Professor Fell and others have offered as proof of ancient contact in the Americas by civilizations beyond the New World.

Grave Creek, Moundsville, West Virginia

In 1838, A. B. Tomlinson excavated a supposed Indian burial mound on property that had been in his family for generations. Five years later, *American Pioneer* published a letter from Mr. Tomlinson describing his excavation of this important site. Here in part is what Mr. Tomlinson had to say:

The flats of Grave Creek are a large scope of bottom land in Marshall County, Virginia ... on the eastern shore of the Ohio River.... The creeks themselves doubtless derived their names from various tumulus or mounds, commonly called Indian graves, which are found on these flats, and especially between the two creeks. Little Grave Creek enters the flats at the upper end and runs parallel with the Ohio about three miles, and then turns at right angles and enters the river one mile above Big Creek....

The flats were early settled. My grandfather settled on them in 1772 ....Elizabethtown is about twelve miles below Wheeling, and is situated on the second bottom, near the mouth of Little Grave Creek, and at the widest part of the flats....

In the suburbs of Elizabethtown stands what is called the mammoth mound, which with its contents is made the subject of this narrative. The mound is surrounded by various other mounds and ancient works, and in respect to the surrounding localities, the situation, as respects defense was well chosen, on the brow of the second bottom, and partially encompassed by steeps and ravines. The mammoth mound is sixty-nine feet high. [Its] circumference at the base is over three-hundred yards.... [It] has a flat top of fifty feet in diameter. This flat on top of the mound, until lately, was dish shaped. The depth of the depression in the center was three feet, and its width forty feet. This depression was doubtless occasioned by the falling in of two vaults, which were originally constructed in the mound, but which afterwards fell in; the earth sinking over them, occasioned the depression on the top.

Tomlinson continues with his letter, establishing the antiquity of the site by noting that his grandfather had discovered it. The mound at that time had a large beech tree growing on top in the center of the depression, and the tree bore inscriptions with dates as early as 1734. A five hundred-year-old white oak also stood on top of the mound, its age determined by counting growth rings after it was cut down.

On March 19, 1838, Tomlinson and companions began digging a horizontal tunnel into the side of the mound. This was no minor-league tunneling operation—they cut a tunnel ten-feet high and seven-feet wide into the mound following the "natural surface of the ground or floor of the mound." Tomlinson's narrative continues:

> At the distance of one hundred and eleven feet we came to a vault that had been excavated in the natural earth before the mound was commenced. This vault was dug out eight by twelve feet square and seven feet deep. Along each side and the two ends upright timbers were placed, which supported timbers that were thrown across the vault, and formed for a time its ceiling. These timbers were covered over with loose unhewn stone, of the same quality as is common in the neighborhood. These timbers rotted, and the stone tumbled into the vault; the earth of the mound following, quite filled it…. This vault was as dry as any tight room; its sides very nearly corresponded with the cardinal points of the compass, and it was lengthwise from north to south.
>
> In this vault were found two human skeletons, one of which had no ornaments or artificial work of any kind about it. The other was surrounded by six hundred and fifty ivory beads, and an ivory ornament about six-inches long of the shape, [a figure attached to the letter shows a baton-shaped piece, slightly flared at the center, with two holes bored in

the center]. *It is one- and five-eighths-inches wide in the middle, and half an inch wide at the ends.... The first skeleton we found in the 4ᵗʰ of April, and the second on the 16ᵗʰ, but I shall speak more particularly on these further on.*

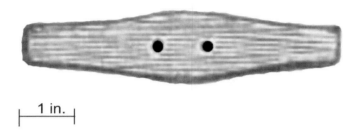

Ivory baton-shaped artifact from Grave Creek

Tomlinson and his crew then dug a ten-foot diameter shaft vertically up through the center of this vault. At thirty-four feet above the vault bottom, he found another vault, more or less equidistant between the lower vault and the top of the mound. They reached that second vault on June 9ᵗʰ. Tomlinson reported that the second vault appeared to be built in the same manner as the lower one. He continued:

> *In the upper vault was found one skeleton only, but many trinkets, as seventeen hundred ivory beads, five hundred sea shells of the involute species, that were worn as beads, and* **five copper bracelets** *that were about the wrist bones of the skeleton. There were also one hundred and fifty pieces of* [mica] **and the stone, a facsimile drawing of which I send you herewith.** *The stone is flat on both sides, and is about three-eighths of an inch thick. It has no engraving on it, except on one side, as sent to you.... The bracelets are of pure*

copper, coated with rust as thick as brown paper. They are an oblong circle. The inner diameter of one is two and one-fourth inches one way, and two and five-eighths the other. They vary in size and thickness.... They were made of round bars bent so that the ends came together, which forms the circle.... [Emphasis added].

This mound, excavated by Mr. Tomlinson, is now part of the West Virginia park system. They state that it is the largest known Adena Indian mound. They estimate that it was built between 250 and 150 BCE.

Mr. Tomlinson's care and precision in his excavation of this mound stands out as exceptional for this period of the early nineteenth century. Fortunately he drew a picture of the engraving on the stone and later the Smithsonian Institution received a cast replica of the stone, because the original stone has been lost.

Grave Creek Stone

Not long after the stone's discovery, Professor Charles C. Rafn, Secretary of the Royal Society of Antiquaries in Denmark, determined that the inscription on the Grave Creek stone was written in an Iberian alphabet, but could not translate it. Then, a number of eminent scientists charged that the inscription was a fraud or hoax. Others came to defend it as an authentic artifact, with many theories of its provenance.

Finally, Professor Fell concluded that the alphabet used on the stone is Punic (Phoenician), consistent with the Semitic writing of that culture in Spain during the first millennium BCE. He translates the engraving as, "the mound raised on high for Tasach. This tile his queen caused to be made." Fell's translation essentially agrees with an independent examination of the engraving by Spanish and other scholars. Donal Buchanan offered this slightly different translation, "Tumulus in honor of Tadach. His wife caused this engraved tile to be inscribed."

As will be seen in the Bat Creek episode, testing those five copper bracelets also recovered by Tomlinson might reveal more about the origin of Tadach. Chemical composition might show that they also came from outside the Native American culture. We are left with many questions about the Grave Creek mound: who was buried there, when were they buried, were Native Americans even involved with this, the "largest Adena mound"?

Based on the presence of the engraved stone, it would appear that the mound builders came from the Iberian Peninsula, and that Tadach, whoever he was, and his wife probably were buried there. Access to the skeletal remains, the original stone, and the bracelets would help answer these questions, but that is no longer possible one hundred and seventy years after the discovery.

Horse Creek Petroglyph

Also in West Virginia near Lynco in Boone County, the Horse Creek petroglyph gives more evidence of ancient visitors to the New World. The purported date for this rock inscription is 600 to 700 CE. The inscription in Ogham, curiously arranged to depict a bison, has yielded a number of translations with little or no similarity. Professor Barry Fell first translated the inscription believing that the Ogham

Q C T D H N S F L B

P R Z NG G M

I E U O A

Ogham Alphabet

Ogham Stone near Dún Aengus Fort, Aran Isles Letters highlighted in white

letters should be assumed to represent letters in the Old Irish and Berber alphabet. His translation provides a reference to Christmas, the virgin birth, and other clearly Christian texts.

Edo Nyland, writing in *Linguistic Archaeology,* offered a much different and more plausible translation after deciding that the Ogham script represented the Basque language. His translation gives an account of an encounter with a frightened herd of bison stampeded into a ravine and then slaughtered by the people leaving this inscription. The inscription is signed by *Iaguntxo*, which translates to "your good friend."

This inscription did not receive scholarly examination until Professor Fell published his conclusions about the petroglyph and his tentative translation in an issue of *Wonderful West Virginia* magazine in 1983. Since that time, scholars have generally agreed that the inscription is genuine Ogham, of the date estimated, and clearly implies a presence other than the Native Americans in West Virginia.

This inscription, according to Nyland, may be the longest Ogham inscription ever found in the world. He also suggests the author of the inscription may have been a "Gnostic Christian Monk."

The Bat Creek Stone

In February, 1889, a Civil War veteran working for the Smithsonian Institution conducted archaeological surveys of a series of mounds lying along the valley of the Little Tennessee River. In one of the mounds he found nine skeletons. Under the head of one of them he found a stone bearing what appeared to be an inscription. He also recovered two "copper" bracelets associated with this skeleton. Modern metallurgical analysis has revealed that those bracelets are made of brass—an alloy Native Americans did not produce. In fact, the particular brass composition compares favorably to brass known to have been smelted during the first two centuries CE in the Old World.

As to the inscription, the Smithsonian concluded that the text was Cherokee. However, Sequoyah did not invent the Cherokee alphabet until about 1820, consequently, the text, if

Cherokee, could not date back sixteen centuries before Sequoyah. There the matter rested until Cyrus Gordon at Brandeis University took a look at the inscription in the 1960s. He determined that the previous scholars had the inscription upside down. When examined right side up, the characters appeared to Gordon to be an old Hebrew script, one used about the time of Christ. Thus the inscription and the brass bracelets appear to tie the Bat Creek site to possible Judean visitors from the Mediterranean region.

Bat Creek Stone

The ubiquitous Professor Barry Fell also has taken a look at the Bat Creek artifacts and related skeletal remains from Eastern Tennessee sites. He asserts that skeletal remains show the mixing of typical Indian individuals with European skeletal remains at these sites. He points out that a radio-carbon date for the Bat Creek inscription indicates that it was placed in the ground about 1,650 +/- 170 years ago. Taking the upper limit of that range, the object would date to about 180 CE—consistent with the linguistic analysis dating it to the early Christian period.

Fell and Gordon agree that the letters spell out the phrase "for the Jews" or "for Judea." Fell adds the words "a comet" to the beginning of the phrase. *Numbers 24.17* contains a prophecy that "'a star shall come forth out of Jacob; a scepter shall rise out of Israel." The Jews thus believed that a star or comet would herald their successful revolt against the tyranny of the Romans in the second century after Christ.

If genuine and accurately dated, the Bat Creek inscription shows the presence of Jewish travelers along the Tennessee River network about 1,700 or 1,800 years ago.

Libyan Tablet in Ecuador

Father Carlo Crespi, a Milanese Catholic priest, lived among the Indians in Cuenca in the Ecuadorian highlands for nearly sixty years (1923-1982). As he gained their trust, they began to bring him artifacts that they said they found in extensive cave networks there. As a huge quantity of these artifacts began to grow, Father Crespi transferred them to a museum he had built. He recognized that these artifacts came from many different cultures, and those cultures were not native to Ecuador or even to the Americas. I have chosen two from hundreds to discuss here.

The first is a stone plaque, triangular in shape, inscribed with a sun symbol at the top, an elephant drawn below the sun, and below that, three lines of script. The text reads, "The elephant that supports the Earth upon the waters and causes it to quake."

The script is Libyan, dating to about 180 BCE. How this plaque came to the possession of the Indians of Cuenca, Ecuador, remains a mystery. That they could have fabricated it as a forgery to palm off on the credulous priest seems unlikely. How could uneducated Indians have known how to inscribe ancient Libyan letters and combine them with the appropriate drawing of the elephant? Such a scenario is unlikely, leaving the conclusion that the plaque must have come to Ecuador by some other means. Archaeologists say that the earliest occupation of this region—dating before the Incas—occurred about 500 CE.

Plaque from Fr. Crespi's collection with Libyan Inscription

Assuming the story told by the priest and the Indians is true, at some point Libyan voyagers came to this region of Ecuador. Some archaeologists would have us believe that the artifact, if it is genuine—and some would insist that it is not—was discarded by a modern day collector or perhaps brought to Ecuador by Spanish conquistadors. The logical conclusion seems the most likely—Libyans visited Ecuador and left this religious tablet there. Collectors seldom abandon valuable artifacts, and the Spaniards who settled this region would not likely have had such items in their possession.

The next artifact from Father Crespi's collection is a stone tablet with a bas relief carving of typical Middle-Eastern design. It bears no resemblance to indigenous American carvings found in Central and South America. It most resembles an Assyrian or Hittite guardian figure of the fourteenth century BCE depicting a human headed bull.

Here again, the local Indians probably did not fabricate this stone figure. How it made its way to Ecuador and into Crespi's collection remains a mystery. We only have his statement that it is one of the many artifacts brought to him from tunnels or caves in the region.

14th Century BCE Assyrian or Hittite Bas Relief

Were the collections of Father Crespi the only anomalous artifacts to turn up in the Americas, we could dismiss them as archaeologists do—discarded collectibles brought here by Spaniards or other modern travelers, or deliberate forgeries and hoaxes. However, when taken with the messages chiseled in stone at remote locations, many of which were first discovered two centuries ago, in languages and forms of writing not deciphered until the twentieth century, it becomes difficult to argue against visits to the New World by cultures dating back four thousand years. These Libyan, Hebrew, Phoenician, Iberian Celtic, Irish Celtic, Basque, and Norse explorers and traders left their marks across the Americas in the form of messages, constructions of tumuli, stone buildings, astronomical sites, and even left their human remains along with grave goods such as the brass bracelets in Tennessee.

Chapter 7
Iarghalan

Irish monks writing during the twelfth century referred to ancient stories of a land across the vast sea—*Iarghalan*. Iarghalan is Gaelic for "land beyond the sunset." In the previous chapter we learned about a biblical account of joint voyages by Phoenicians and Israelites that may have reached America based on a religious inscription in New Mexico. Phoenicians clearly had a strong presence in the Iberian Peninsula. The earliest invaders of Ireland (ancient name Ibheriu) came from the Iberian Peninsula or Iberia— pronounced very nearly the same as Ibheriu. They were Celts who had moved into the same area of Iberia as the Phoenicians and had blended their cultures.

The Celtic invaders of Ireland would have brought with them their legend of earlier voyages to the land beyond the sunset. According to Irish legend, in the sixth century Irish monks sailed to the New World. We do not know where they supposedly landed. They were led by St. Brendan who was born in 484 at Ciarraighe Luachra near present-day Tralee. He died in 577 at Annaghdown, Galway.

Brendan studied under St. Ita and St. Erc in Munster and was ordained a priest in 512. He established monastic cells at various locations and became abbot of the monastery of Shanakeel. He left on his seven-year voyage from that monastery. When he returned, he created another monastery in County Clare and then traveled to Wales and Iona in Britain. After three years there, he returned to Ireland and spent his remaining days there building churches and monasteries in various locales. He was buried at Clonfert Abbey, one of his creations.

Navagatio sancti Brendani abbatis, written by the tenth century, tells of St. Brendan's voyage to find Tír na nÓg, the land of eternal youth believed to be far to the west. According to this account, Brendan did not claim to be the first to complete such a voyage. He learned of this land from Father Barinthus who visited Brendan and his monks and told the story of Mernoc, another Irish monk who had left Barinthus's flock to live a solitary life on an island, the Island of Delights (location unknown). Other monks had followed Mernoc to this isolated cloister. Barinthus sailed to the Island of Delights and then he joined Mernoc in a voyage to the Land of Promise of the Saints—the mythical land beyond the sunset.

St. Brendan depicted in a 15th Century German manuscript

This tale of Barinthus and Mernoc inspired Brendan to plan for a voyage himself to the Land of Promise of the Saints. Brendan chose fourteen monks to accompany him; three more would join him at the last minute before his departure from Ireland.

Brendan had a large boat built, consisting of a wooden frame of oak covered with tanned ox hides. The boat builders waterproofed the sewn seams of the ox hides with animal fat. This boatbuilding technique is still used today in Celtic regions to construct capable sea-going craft.

After a forty-day period of prayer and fasting, Brendan cast off from the southwest coast of Ireland from a creek that now bears his name. They sailed first to the Aran Islands off Galway where they stopped for a few days, then set out for the great unknown sea to the north.

Brendan and his monks made landfall on a series of islands as they sailed north, finding inhabitants on most of them. They sailed, rowed, and at times allowed the craft to drift with the prevailing winds and tides, trusting that God would direct them on their quest. According to the colorful language of this medieval tale, they encountered sea monsters and demons as well as saintly persons. They were helped by a mystical dog, birds, a hermit, and numerous monks living on remote islands. Here's one of the more fantastical passages:

The saint sailed forth into the ocean, and the boat was borne along for the space of forty days. One day a fish of enormous size appeared swimming after the boat, spouting foam from its nostrils, and plowing through the waves in rapid pursuit to devour them. Then the brethren cried out to the lord: "O Lord, who hast made us, O Father, help us;" and to St.

Brendan they cried aloud: "Help Oh father, help us;" and the saint besought the Lord to deliver His servants, that this monster might not devour them, while he also sought to give courage to the brethren in these words: "Fear not, you of little faith, for God, who is always our protector, will deliver us from the jaws of this monster, and from every other danger." When the monster was drawing near, waves of immense size rushed on before it, even up to the gunwale of the boat, which caused the brethren to fear more and more; but St. Brendan, with his hands upraised to heaven, earnestly prayed: "Deliver, O Lord, Thy servants, as Thou didst deliver David from the hands of the giant Goliath, and Jonas from the power of the great whale." When these prayers were uttered, a great monster came into view from the west, and rushing against the other, spouting flame from its mouth, at once attacked it. Then St. Brendan spoke: "Behold, my children, the wonderful work of our Savior; see here the obedience of the creature to its Creator: await now the end in safety, for this conflict will bring no evil to us, but only greater glory to God." Thereupon the rueful monster that pursued the servants of God is slain, and cut up in their presence into three parts, and its victor returned whence it came.

This passage appears to be mere fantasy and could make the modern-day reader doubt the validity of any of St. Brendan's tale. However, when we decipher the medieval narrative style in Brendan's tale, we can find logical explanations for most of what he relates. In this case, the monks apparently witnessed a clash between a whale and some other large marine mammal or fish—perhaps a great white shark. Such conflicts do take place and perhaps that is what Brendan and his monks saw.

In another episode of his tale, the monks apparently saw a volcanic eruption from a North Atlantic island. They described molten slag hurled toward them from the island. In the narrative, demonic smiths have thrown glowing embers at them, but that rather colorful description may be merely the transformation the actual episode went through as it was told and retold over a period of one hundred or more years.

After seven years of island hopping around the North Atlantic, St. Brendan took on a guide, identified only as their "procurator", and after forty days of sailing, they reached the land they sought.

> *When they had disembarked, they saw a land, extensive and thickly set with trees laden with fruits, as in the autumn season. All the time they were traversing that land, during their stay in it, no night was there, but a light always shone, like the light of the sun in the meridian, and for the forty days they viewed the land in various directions, they could not find the limits thereof.*

Brendan's tale contains a prophecy near the end:

> *After many years this land will be made manifest to those who come after you, when days of tribulation may come upon the people of Christ …. When the Most High Creator will have brought all nations under subjection, then will this land be made known to all His elect.*

The excerpts quoted above come from the Latin version of Brendan's Tale translated into English by Denis O'Donoghue in 1893. The complete translation can be read on-line at The Celtic Christianity e-Library thanks to Jonathan M. Wooding.

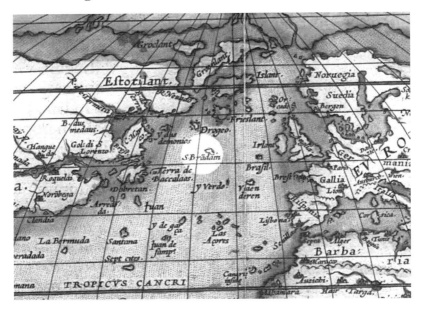

St. Brendan's Isle was shown on early maps of the Atlantic
This one shows the isle (highlighted in white) on a map of 1570

But did St. Brendan really reach North America? We will never know for sure that he did, but we can be sure that he could have. In 1976, Tim Severin, a man who delights in recreating legendary voyages, built a hide-covered boat following the description in St. Brendan's Tale, and using other known examples of sixth-century Celtic boat building techniques. He went to great pains to select the correct wood, hides, and tanning techniques to obtain materials that are considered typical of what St. Brendan would have used. Severin also used period tools and fabrication techniques to ensure that his boat was as faithful a replica as possible.

Bishop of Kerry, Eammon Casey, christened the vessel *Brendan* with a bottle of Irish whiskey

Tim Severin's *Brendan*
A reconstructed hide–covered ship

Severin set out from St. Brendan's Creek (aka. Brandon Creek) on May 17, 1976 with a crew of half a dozen adventurers rather than the eighteen monks of the original voyage. They took their time learning how the boat sailed and stopped at the Aran Isles, St. MacDara's Isle, and Ballyhoorisky in Northern Ireland before continuing on to Iona, and the Hebrides. So far, they had seldom been out of sight of land. Leaving the Hebrides on June 18, they sailed for more than 300 miles through open waters to the Faroes, making landfall there on June 24th.

Their course up to that point had been northerly. From the Faroes, they sailed west to Iceland, putting into Reykjavik on July 16th. This leg of their journey took them 640 miles in open ocean conditions. *Brendan* had performed outstandingly from a seaworthiness perspective. It was not the most maneuverable boat, certainly, but they were not in danger of sinking. At times, like St. Brendan, they had to let the boat go where the wind and tide directed it, but the prevailing conditions carried them toward their destination. They remained in Iceland for the winter.

At the Hebrides and the Faroes, they found evidence and heard tales of the medieval Irish monks who had arrived there centuries before to establish monasteries and farms on the islands. There can be little doubt that the Irish as well as even earlier cultures had the capability to reach those islands of the North Atlantic and had settled there. The islands referred to by St. Brendan probably were those that make up the Hebrides and the Faroes as well as Iceland.

On May 8, 1977, Severin and his crew sailed away from Iceland on a westerly course headed for North America. After about a week of making good progress, they found themselves stymied by adverse wind and current and essentially sailed in circles for about a week before they regained a steady westerly course. By May 28th, they were off the southern tip of Greenland and less than one month later, they made landfall near Gander, Newfoundland. They had covered about 1,600 miles of open ocean since leaving Iceland.

The only serious mishap, one that turned out to be readily handled, was a tear in the hide covering of the boat when they sailed too close to an ice floe. They had spare ox hide on board, and sewed a patch onto the hull while at sea. The repair was arduous in the frigid water, but well-within their ability.

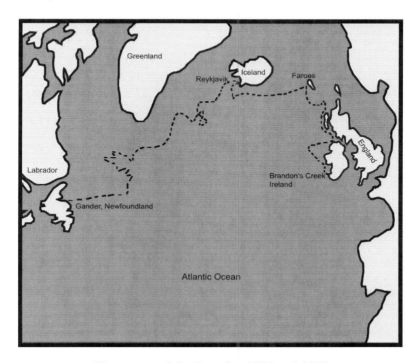

The course of the *Brendan* 1976 and 1977

Severin established a number of important points with this re-enactment of St. Brendan's voyage:

- Hide covered boats could easily sail across the North Atlantic
- Those boats could handle stormy sea conditions
- The prevailing winds and currents during the spring and summer months would carry those boats to the Hebrides, Faroes, Iceland, Greenland and on to Newfoundland

- Had they wanted to, Severin and his crew could have sailed and rowed farther south along the North American coast.

We don't know whether St. Brendan set foot on the North American continent, but it was certainly possible. From his own account, he told that at least two Irishmen had gone before him: Barinthus and Mernoc. They were, according to legend, a few of the many Celtic people who had visited the New World and perhaps by no means the earliest as we know from the preceding chapter.

Chapter 8
Vinland

The Saga of Eric the Red begins with a genealogy of Viking names that evoke the spirit of those sea rovers: Halfdan Whiteleg, Ketil Flatnose, Bjorn the Ungartered, Eystein the Rattler and, my favorite, Thorfinn the Skullcleaver. Having raided and pillaged Ireland, half of Scotland, and the outlying islands, these Vikings, then a bit more civilized, went on to Iceland where they established farming communities.

From about 800 to 1300 CE, the Earth experienced a warming climate in the Northern hemisphere, pushing back the glacial expanses and making Northern Europe and the North Atlantic regions more temperate. In the second half of the ninth century, those Norse settlers arrived at Iceland. Imagine their surprise when they found the presence of Irish monks already there.

The earliest Icelandic book recording settlement there identifies a Viking named Naddoddr as the first to land there. He called the place the Land of Snow and promptly went home. Others followed, and by 930 CE Iceland had a stable population occupying all of the arable land. *The Saga of Eric the Red* tells us:

> *There was a man named Thorvald,.... His son was named Eirik. Father and son removed from Jadar* [Norway] *because of manslaughters, and occupied land in Hornstrandir, and dwelt at Drangar. There Thorvald died, and Eirik then married Thjohild, daughter of Jorund ... and Thorbjorg the Ship-Breasted .... Eirik slew Eyjolf the Foul; he slew also Hrafn the kinsman of Eyholf....* [after yet more killings]

95

> *Eirik and his people were outlawed at Thorsnes Thing. He*
> *prepared a ship in Eiriksvagr, and … said to his people that*
> *he purposed to seek for the land which Gunnbjorn … saw*
> *when he was driven westwards over the ocean, and discovered*
> *Guubjarnarsker* [Gunnbjorn's rock]…. *Eirik went to live*
> *in the land which he had discovered, and which he called*
> *Greenland, "Because," said he, "men will desire much the more*
> *to go there if the land has a good name."*

Thus began the time-honored profession of grandiose names
for real estate developments.

Eric the Red in fanciful armor
From a 1688 Icelandic woodcut

96

Eric the Red's father had left Norway because of some inconvenient "manslaughters" and Eric had to leave Iceland after one too many killings of his neighbors—the last supposedly over a disputed shovel. He opened Greenland for subsequent Viking settlement.

Eric the Red discovers Greenland

About 986, Biarne Herjulfsson sailed from Iceland to visit with his father in Greenland. He had not made this trip before. *The Flatey Book*, a collection of sagas, describes Biarne's voyage:

> *But yet put they now out to sea, as soon as they were ready, and sailed for three days, until the land was hidden under the water; but the fair wind failed, and changed into north-winds and fogs, and knew they not whither they went, and lasted this many days. Thereafter got they sight of the sun, and could distinguish the [course]; hoist now sail, and sail that day, ere they saw land, and deliberated with each other, what land that might be; and Biarne professed to think, that might not be Greenland. They ask, whether he will sail to this land or not.*

It is my counsel to sail close to the land. And so do they, and saw that soon, that the land was mountain-less and wood-grown and small hills on the land; and left the land on larboard and let the sheet turn toward land. They ask, whether Biarne supposed this was Greenland yet.

He quoth no more to think this to be Greenland than the former. For glaciers are very large said to be in Greenland. They approached soon this land and saw it to be flat land and widely wooded. Then failed the fair wind them. Then uttered the men, that to them seemed best to take to land, but Biarne will not. They pretended to lack both wood and water. Of neither of these are you unprovided, says Biarne; but, though, got he for this some blame from his men. He bade them hoist sail, and so was done, and set the stem from the land and sail to sea with south-westerly wind for three days, and saw them the third land, and this land was high and mountainous and with glaciers on it. They ask then, if Biarne would land lay there, but he quoth, he would not, because to me appears this land unprofitable.

Now they did not lower their sail, go ahead along the land and saw that it was an island, set again the stern toward this land and hold out to sea with the same fair wind, but the wind waxed at once, and bade Biarne then to reef, and not sail faster than both would suit well their ship and rigging. Sailed now for four days. Then saw they land, the fourth. Then asked they Biarne, whether he thought this to be Greenland or not. Biarne answers: this is likest that, which to me has been told about Greenland, and here may we to the land steer. So they do and take land below some ness [cape or headland] *at eve-tide. And from him the ness has taken name, and is afterwards called Heriulf's ness. Went Biarne now to his father. And gives now up his sailing and stays with his father, while Heriulf lived, and afterward dwelt he there after his father.*

The three lands Biarne accidentally sailed to and rejected before finding Greenland were probably Labrador, Newfoundland, and what later became Vinland.

While in Greenland, Biarne visited with Eric the Red, Earl of Greenland. Biarne told of his sailing from Iceland, being blown off course, and discovery of other lands farther west and south of Greenland. *The Greenlander's Saga* continues the story:

> *Was there now much speaking of land-seeking. Leif, son of Eric the Red from Brattalid, went to visit Biarne Herjulfsson and bought ship of him, and hired a crew, so that there were three tens and a half men together* [thirty-five men]. *Leif begged his father Eric, if he would a leader be on the expedition. Eric excused himself, said he was too old in age and said he could not endure the troubles of the sea as before. Leif said he yet might with best luck rule them, the kinsmen, and then Eric yielded to Leif and rode from home, when they were ready, and there was not far to go to the ship. The horse stumbled, which Eric rode, and fell he off from its back and hurt his foot, then quoth Eric: not is for me fated to find more lands than this where we now dwell, we now no longer may follow together.*

Was this fall from the horse staged by Eric to avoid the trip? We'll never know. In any case, Leif pressed on with his expedition to the west.

> *… Leif went to the ship and his fellows with him. There was a southern man with them, who Tyrker was called. Now they built their ship and went to sea, when they had finished,*

and found then that land first, which Biarne found last. There sailed they to land and cast anchor and put out the boat and went ashore and saw there no grass, large ice mountains were seen far away but like one stone field was all to the ice mountains from the sea, and seemed to them this land to be good for nothing. Then quoth Leif: not to us has it happened with this land as to Biarne that we have not got upon the land. Now I will give name to the land and call it Helluland. Afterwards they went to ship, and then sailed they on the sea and found another land, sail again to land and cast anchor, then put out the boat and get ashore that land was level and wood-covered and wide white sands wherever they went and not steep at the shore. Then quoth Leif: After its quality shall this land have name, and be called Markland. Went after that to the ship as fast as possible.

Now sailed they from thence on the sea before a northeast and were out for two days, ere they saw land, and sailed to this land and came to an island, which lay to the north of the land, and went up there and looked about in fine weather and found that there was a dew on the grass, and it happened to them, that they touched the dew with their hands and brought it to their mouths, and thought not to have known anything so sweet as this was. Afterwards they went to their ship and sailed into a sound that lay between the island and that cape which went to the north from the land, steering to the west of the cape, there was very shallow at ebb-tide, and stood there aground their ship and was there far to the sea to see from the ship. Yet they were so very curious to go ashore that they could not bide that the high water would rise under their ship, but ran to the land, where a river fell into the sea from a lake. But as soon as the

*tide rose under their ship, they took the boat and rowed to the
ship and conveyed it up the river, afterwards into the lake and
cast there anchor and brought from the ship their leather bags
and made there booths, took that resolution afterwards to abide
there for that winter and made there a large house. Neither
wanted there salmon in the river nor in the lake, and larger
salmon than they had before seen.*

Leif Eriksson discovers America

From this base of operations, Leif and his men explored
their island and points to the south. One of the explorers was
an older man, Tyrker, who spoke a "southern tongue." We do
not know where he came from, perhaps somewhere in
Europe. Tyrker had been away too long, and Leif sent a
dozen men to search for him. Soon they returned with a very
excited Tyrker.

*He spoke then first a long time in his southern tongue and
rolled much his eyes and made wry faces, but they did not*

understand what he said, he spoke then in northern language after a while. I have walked not much farther, yet I can something curious relate: I found wine trees and wine berries. May that be true, foster-father mine, quoth Leif. To be sure it is true, quoth he, for I was there born, where neither vine nor grapes are scarce. Now slept they through that night; but the next morning Leif said to his crew: now we shall have two works, and shall every day either gather grapes or cut vines and fell timber, so that they may be a lading for my ship; and this advice was taken. So is said, that their aft-boat was filled with grapes. Now was hewn a landing for the ship. And when spring came, they made ready and sailed away; and gave Leif name to the land after the lands products and called it Wineland. Sailed now after that to sea and got fair wind, until they saw Greenland ....

Modern versions of the Leif Ericsson story call the land Vinland. He had his father's knack for naming prospective real estate developments. Leif's first voyage to Vinland took place about the year 1000 CE. Eric the Red died the winter that Leif returned to Greenland. Leif's brother, Thorvald, led the next voyage of thirty men to Vinland to continue its exploration and to bring more timber to Greenland—Leif had returned from Vinland on the first voyage with timber as well as grapes.

Thorvald said that they should make their ship ready, and should the aft-boat of the ship and some men with it go to the western part of the land and explore there during the summer. To them seemed the land fair and wooded, and not far from the woods to the sea and the white sands; there were many islands and shallows. They found dwellings neither of men nor of beasts, but in one of the western islands they found a corn-shed of wood, not found they more works of man, and went back and came to Leif's booths at harvest time. But the next summer, Thorvald went eastwards with the merchant ship, and to the north of the land. Then came upon them a hard weather off a ness, and were driven on shore there and broke the keel under the ship, and had there a long delay and mended their ship.

Then said Thorvald to his followers: now I will, that we raise here up the keel on the ness and call it Kialnar Ness, and so they did. Afterwards they sail from thence away and to the east of the land and into the firth-mouth, that was there next to it, and to a headland, which sprang forth there; it was all wood-grown; there they make first their ship fast, and put out the gang-board to the shore, and goes Thorvald there on shore with all his followers. Quoth he then: here is fair, and here would I raise my abode.

Went afterwards to the ship and saw on the sands within the headland three hills, and went there and saw there three leather boats and three men under each of them. Then they divided their party and laid hand on them all but one, who escaped with his boat. They kill those eight and go afterwards on the headland and looked about, and saw up the firth some hills, and supposed they those to be settlements.

After that they were stricken with weariness so great that they could not keep awake, and fell they all asleep. Then came a call above them, so that they all awoke. Thus says the call: Awake thou Thorvald and all thy company, if thou wilt keep thy life, and go thou to thy ship with all thy men, and sail from this land as quickly as possible. Then came from within the firth numberless leather boats and made at them. Quoth then

Thorvald: we shall put outboards the shields and defend ourselves as best we may, but attack only little.

So they did, but the Skraelings shot at them for a while and fled afterwards away, as hurriedly as each of them might. Then asked Thorvald his men, if they were anyhow wounded. They answered not to be wounded. I have got a wound under the arm, says he, and flew an arrow between the shipside and the shield under my arm, and here is the arrow, and may me this to death lead, now I advise that you prepare to go as soon as possible back, but you shall bring me to that headland, which I thought most habitable to be, may be, that a true word came of my mouth, that I might dwell there for a while. There you shall bury me and set a cross at my head and at my feet, and call it Krossaness for ever after.

The Vikings buried Thorvald as he had requested, presumably <u>after</u> he had died. They remained there through the winter gathering more grapes and cutting more timber for their cargo. In the spring, they sailed back to Greenland.

Thorstein, brother of Leif and Thorvald, led the next expedition to Vinland. He planned to go there to retrieve his brother's body and continue the exploration of this new land. His wife Gudrid and twenty-five men joined him on the voyage. But they ran afoul of the weather and made landfall at another Greenland settlement far removed from their home. Thorstein died there during the winter.

Eventually, Gudrid and the remnants of Thorstein's expedition made their way back to Brattalid. She soon found a second husband, Thorfinn Karlsefne. The Vinland story would continue under the leadership of Thorfinn and Gudrid.

They led sixty men and five women on this voyage, making their first landfall at Leif's original encampment.

They got soon in hand a large and good catch, for a whale was driven up there, both large and good; they went hither and cut the whale. Were then not short of food. The cattle went up on the land there, but it soon happened, that the males became unruly and caused much trouble. They had with them one bull. Karlsefne let trees fell and hew for his ship, and laid the wood on a rock for drying. They profited by all the products of the land that there were, both of grapes and deer and fish and all good things. After this first winter came summer, they became aware of Skraelings, and came there out from the wood a great troop of men. There was near cattle of theirs, and the bull took to bellow and roar extremely, but this frightened the Skraelings, and they ran away with their burdens, but those were grey fur and sable and all sorts of skin-wares; and they turned towards Karlsefne's abode and would there enter the houses; but Karlsefne made defend the doors. Neither understood the other's language.

Then the Skraelings took down their packs and loosened them, and offered them and desired weapons especially for them, but Karlsefne forbade them to sell weapons, and now he takes the counsel, that he bade the women carry out milk to them, and as soon as they saw the milk, then would they buy that and nothing else. Now was this the purchasing of the Skraelings, that they carried their bargain away in their stomachs. But Karlsefne and his followers kept their packs and skin-wares. Went they thus away.... At this time, Gudrid, Karlsefne's wife, brought forth a male child, and the boy was called Snorre.

Snorre was therefore the first child of European parents born in America—at least the first we know by name. Snorre beat Virginia Dare into the record book by about 580 years. Soon after Snorre was born, the Skraelings attacked the settlement again. Although the Vikings remained unharmed, Karlsefne decided in the spring to return to Greenland. They returned home with another cargo of timber, grapes, and the animal skins they had bought from the Skraelings.

Next to travel to Vinland was Freydis, Eric the Red's daughter. She convinced two brothers, Helge and Finnboge, who had recently arrived in Greenland from Norway, to sail with her to Vinland. She would split the profit with them. But Freydis had inherited the violent tendency of her grandfather and father. Two ships sailed to Vinland—one carrying Freydis and her husband, the other Helge and Finnboge. Each ship also carried about thirty men, and five women sailed on the brothers' ship.

At Leif's old encampment in Vinland, Freydis soon wreaked havoc on her supposed business partners. She convinced her husband that the brothers had abused her and caused him to murder the brothers and their crew. Then, when the men refused to murder the two brothers' women, Freydis took up an axe and killed the five women. She swore all the men remaining alive to tell a story when they returned to Greenland that the brothers and their crew had opted to remain in Vinland. Then she loaded the larger of the two ships—the one that had been owned by Helge and Finnboge—with goods and sailed back home.

Leif soon learned of his sister's treachery. He confirmed the fact by torturing three of her companions until they told what really had transpired at Vinland. Freydis lived out her life ostracized by the rest of the settlers in Greenland.

An anecdote from *The Saga of Eric the Red* adds just a little bit more to the history of this Viking settlement attempt in North America:

> *Now, when they sailed from Vinland, they had a southern wind, and reached Markland, and found five Skraelings; one was a bearded man, two were women, two children. Karlsefne's people caught the children, but the others escaped and sunk down into the earth. And they took the children with them, and taught them their speech, and they were baptized. The children called their mother Voetilldi, and their father Uvoegi. They said that kings ruled over the land of the Skraelings, one of whom was called Avalldamon, and the other Valldidida. They said also that there were no houses, and the people lived in caves or holes. They said, moreover, that there was a land on the other side over against their land, and the people there were dressed in white garments, uttered loud cries, bare long poles, and wore fringes. This was supposed to be Hvitramannaland* [white man's land].

They also called Hvitramannaland "Great Ireland." The Norse believed at the time of the sagas that Irish monks lived near where Karlsefne had captured the Native American children and that the children's description was of a religious procession in which monks in white carried fringed religious banners on poles.

The Legend of Saguenay

When the French began to colonize Canada the Algonquians told them about a kingdom to the north called Saguenay. According to the Indians that kingdom contained great stores of gold and silver. The people there had blond hair and fair skin.

The legend gained further embellishments when Donnacona, the chief of an Iroquoian village on the St. Lawrence River at present-day Quebec, returned to France with Jacques Cartier in 1535. Donnacona regaled the French court with stories of the kingdom of Saguenay, leading the French to conduct expeditions in search of the legendary region of white men.

Some historians believe that the story of Saguenay was simply an Indian attempt to mislead the French explorers. Others believe that Saguenay embodied memories of Norse explorers in Canada dating back to the time of Leif Eriksson.

The name Saguenay appears on modern maps of Canada as the name of a river in Quebec and other place names.

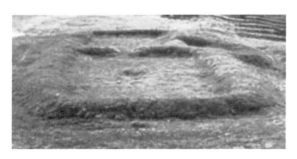

Remains of Viking longhouse

Viking artifacts from L'Anse aux Meadows Stone lamp and cloak pin

For much of the twentieth century, historians treated the sagas of Iceland and Greenland as mythology. They dismissed the idea of Leif Eriksson reaching North America as mere fantasy. Then, in 1960, Norwegian archaeologists Helge and Anne Stine Ingstad discovered irrefutable proof of at least one Norse settlement at the northern tip of Newfoundland. The location, known as L'Anse aux Meadows (Jellyfish Cove), contains the remains of a settlement containing a number of earth and timber longhouses, iron works, and various artifacts of Norse origin dating to the period of Leif Eriksson's voyage.

We cannot say that the archaeologists found Eriksson's first settlement, but it certainly appears in the right locale and dates, as near as can be determined, to the correct period. In time, archaeology will surely disclose more Viking settlement activity along the east coast of North America.

Historians now acknowledge that the Vikings reached America as the sagas describe. The consensus is that Helluland is Labrador, Markland is Newfoundland, and Vinland was farther south—anywhere from Nova Scotia to New York. Perhaps, artifacts will turn up somewhere along that rather extensive stretch of coast that will shed more light on where Vinland was. Until then, the mystery remains.

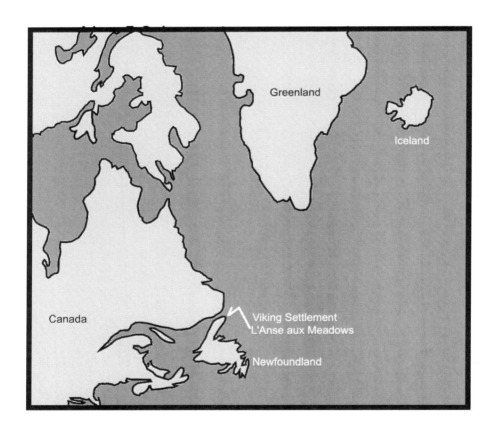

Location of Viking settlement found in Newfoundland

Chapter 9
Welsh Prince Madoc ca. 1170

After the death of [Welsh Prince] *Owen Guyneth, his sonnes fell at debate who should inherit after him: for the eldest sonne borne in matrimony, Edward or Iorweth Drwydion, was counted unmeet to governe, because of the maime upon his face: and Howell that tooke upon him all the rule was a base sonne, begotten upon an Irish woman. Therefore David gathered all the power he could, and came against Howel, and fighting with him, slew him; and afterwards injoyed quietly the whole land of Northwales, until his brother Iorwerths sonne came to age.*

Madoc another of Owen Guyneth his sonnes left the land in contention betwixt his brethren, and prepared certaine ships, with men and munition, and sought adventures by Seas, sailing West, and leaving the coast of Ireland so farre North, that he came unto a land unknowen, where he saw many strange things.

This land must needs be some part of that Countrey of which the Spanyards affirme themselves to be the first finders since Hannos time. Whereupon it is manifest that that countrey was by Britaines discovered, long before Columbus led any Spanyards thither.

Of the voyage and returne of this Madoc there be many fables feined, as the common people doe vse in distance of place and length of time rather to augment then to diminish: but sure it is there he was. And after he had returned home, and declared the pleasant and fruitfull countreys that he had seen without inhabitants, and upon the contrary part, for what barren and wild ground his brethren and nephews did murther one another, he prepared a number of ships, and got with him such men and women as were desirous to live in quietness: and taking leave of his friends, tooke his journey thitherward againe. Therefore it is to be supposed that he and his people inhabited part of those countreys: for it appeareth by Francis Lopez de Gomara, that in Acuzamil [a Mayan city] *and other places the people honored the crosse. Wherby it may be gathered that Christians had bene there before the comming of the Spanyards. But because this people were not many, they followed the maners of the land which they came unto, and used the language they found there.*

This Madoc arriving in that Westerne countrey, unto the which he came in the yere 1170, left most of his people there, and returning backe for more of his owne nation, acquaintance and friends to inhabit that faire and large countrey, went thither againe with ten sailes, as I find noted by Gutyn Owen. I am of opinion that the land whereunto he came was some part of the West Indies.

The above account of Madoc's two colonial expeditions to the New World comes from Rev. Richard Hakluyt, an unabashed sixteenth-century proponent of England's right to settlement of North America. Hakluyt's source was a Welsh poet, Gutyn Owen, who wrote about Madoc about 1480—three hundred years after Madoc lived. However, earlier accounts exist in fragmentary form found on Lundy Island, Madoc's point of departure from Welsh waters, according to Madoc biographer Dana Olson.

Dana Olson described Madoc as tall, handsome, and mild mannered, a man uninterested in the interminable wars that occupied his brothers. Madoc, however, had considerable naval experience. He had commanded ships for his father, Welsh Prince Owain Gwynedd, in war against the English King Henry II. He had also traveled to Ireland, France, Spain, the Mediterranean Sea, and had visited relatives in Scandinavia—Madoc's mother was of Irish and Viking ancestry.

Madoc was an illegitimate son of Owain Gwynedd and Brenda, daughter of Hywell, a Viking lord in Ireland. Madoc was born at Dolwyddlan Castle in Wales circa 1138. He received his education at Harlech Castle. By 1170, Madoc decided to launch a voyage of discovery across the western sea.

The Welsh of the twelfth century had capable sea-going vessels with planked hulls similar to the Viking trading and war ships. The Celtic people had a history of prowess at sea dating far back to the time of Julius Caesar and probably before. Caesar described the Celtic ships as follows:

> *The influence of this state is by far the most considerable of any of the countries on the whole sea coast, because the Veneti* [a Celtic tribe] *both have a very great number of ships, with which they have been accustomed to sail to Britain, and* [thus] *excel the rest in their knowledge and experience of nautical affairs; and as only a few ports lie scattered along that stormy and open sea, of which they are in possession, they hold as tributaries almost all those who are accustomed to traffic in that sea.*

> *For their ships were built and equipped after this manner: the keels were somewhat flatter than those of our ships, whereby they could more easily encounter the shallows and the ebbing of the tide: the prows were raised very high, and in like manner*

the sterns were adapted to the force of the waves and storms which they were formed to sustain. The ships were built wholly of oak, and designed to endure any force and violence whatever; the benches, which were made of planks a foot in breadth, were fastened by iron spikes of the thickness of a man's thumb; the anchors were secured fast by iron chains instead of cables, and for sails they used skins and thin dressed leather. These were used either through their want of canvas and their ignorance of its application, or for this reason, which is more probable, that they thought that such storms of the ocean, and such violent gales of wind could not be resisted by sails, nor ships of such great burden be conveniently enough managed by them.

The encounter of our fleet with these ships was of such a nature that our fleet excelled in speed alone, and the plying of the oars; other things, considering the nature of the place and the violence of the storms, were more suitable and better adapted on their side; for neither could our ships injure theirs with their beaks (so great was their strength), nor on account of their height was a weapon easily cast up to them; and for the same reason they were less readily locked in by rocks. To this was added, that whenever a storm began to rage and they ran before the wind, they both could weather the storm more easily and heave to securely in the shallows, and when left by the tide feared nothing from rocks and shelves: the risk of all which things was much to be dreaded by our ships. From *de Bello Gallico*, written circa 40 BCE.

So we see that 1,200 years before Madoc sailed, the Celts had large ships with wooden planked hulls, described as very similar to the Norse ships of later years, and these ships were fully capable of sailing the open seas and could make great speed under sail before a favorable wind. Whether or not Madoc sailed to America, the Celtic and Viking world of the twelfth century clearly had the capability to do so.

Madoc would have known from his Scandinavian relatives the tales of Eric the Red and Leif Eriksson sailing westward from Iceland and finding Greenland and Vinland. At the time of Madoc's voyages to the New World, he would have heard stories of Icelandic sailors reaching Irland it Mikla—Ireland the Great—also known as White Man's Land, yet another name for some northern portion of North America. One such fragmentary story Madoc would have heard was the saga of Ari Marson, an Icelandic leader blown off course in the tenth century to this new land occupied by Irishmen:

> *He was driven by a tempest to White Man's Land, which some call Great Ireland; it lies to the west in the sea, near to Vinland the Good .... From thence could Ari not get away, and was there baptized. The story was first told to Rafn the Limerick merchant, who had long lived at Limerick in Ireland.*
>
> *Now are there, as is said, south from Greenland, which is inhabited, deserts, uninhabited places, and ice-bergs, then the Skraelings, then Markland, then Vinland The Good; next, and somewhat behind, lies Albania* [not modern-day Albania], *which is White Man's Land; thither was sailing, formerly, from Ireland; there Irishmen and Icelanders recognized Ari, the son of Mar and Katla of Reykjaness, of whom nothing had been heard for a long time, and who had been made a chief there by the inhabitants.* From *Landnamabok*, the story of the settlement of Iceland.

Albania, also known as White Man's Land, was a mainland across the sea believed to lie near Vinland. From the sagas we know that Vinland was somewhere on the northeast portion of North America south of Newfoundland where Leif Eriksson first landed. White Man's Land was also synonymous with Ireland the Great (not to be confused with Ireland today).

The bards told a similar story of Bjarni Asbrandson, likewise blown off course, making landfall in Ireland the Great, and being elevated to chief there over Irish-speaking people. Bjarni sailed away in 999, never to return to Iceland. In 1029, Gudlief Gudlangson ended up blown ashore in Ireland the Great and met an old chief who refused to give his identity. From a ring and sword given to Gudlief, people in Iceland identified the mysterious chief as the missing Bjarni Asbrandson.

The point of these stories is not whether they were true, but that Madoc and others of his time would have heard those tales of a fabulous mainland or continent, occupied in part by Irish-speaking people, across the western sea. They would not have confused that fabulous land with the Ireland they knew to be a short sail across the narrow sea separating Wales from Ireland.

Theories abound about whether Madoc sailed twice to America, but in the last more than eight hundred years, his story has persisted. Richard Hakluyt, writing in the late sixteenth century, encouraged Queen Elizabeth to grant charters for English settlement of North America in part on the strength of the claim that Madoc ap Gwynedd had reached North America long before Columbus gave the Spanish a claim on the land.

The Spanish had heard the story of Madoc's voyages to and settlement of North America. In fact, Christopher Columbus noted on the margin of one of his maps of the West Indies that those waters were Welsh waters, clearly recognizing that Madoc had gone there before him. The Spanish would look for and find signs of the Welsh or other Christians having preceded them in the Americas. They would do their best to eradicate any evidence of a Welsh priority since their Papal charter to the New World rested on the belief that they were the first Christians to set foot in the New World.

Peter Martyr of Anghiera, an historian working for the Spanish king in the early 16th century, writing about the earliest Spanish explorations of the Yucatan Peninsula, reported that "Crosses have been seen amongst them [the Maya]; and when they were asked, through interpreters, the meaning of that emblem, some of them answered that a very beautiful man had once lived amongst them, who had left them this symbol as a remembrance of him; others said that a man more radiant than the sun had died upon that cross." Martyr, who had access to Christopher Columbus and his papers, is also the source of the notation Columbus made about "Welsh waters" in the West Indies. The Spanish clearly saw signs that the Welsh or some other Christian explorers had visited Mexico and influenced the Indians there. Here in part is Martyr's account of Columbus's first voyage and landfall:

Upon leaving these islands [Canaries] *and heading straight to the west, with a slight deviation to the south-west, Columbus sailed thirty-three successive days without seeing anything but sea and sky. His companions began to murmur in secret, for at first they concealed their discontent, but soon, openly, desiring to get rid of their leader, whom they even planned to throw into the sea. They considered that they had been deceived by this Genoese, who was leading them to some place from whence they could never return.*

After the thirtieth day they angrily demanded that he should turn back and go no farther; Columbus, by using gentle words, holding out promises and flattering their hopes, sought to gain time, and he succeeded in calming their fears; finally also reminding them that if they refused him their obedience or attempted violence against him, they would be accused of treason by their sovereigns. To their great joy, the much-desired land was finally discovered.

During this first voyage Columbus visited six islands, two of which were of extraordinary magnitude; one of these he named Hispaniola, and the other Juana, [Cuba] *though he was not positive that the latter was an island. While sailing along the coasts of these islands, in the month of November, the Spaniards heard nightingales singing in the dense forests, and they discovered great rivers of fresh water, and natural harbors sufficient for the largest fleets. Columbus reconnoitered the coast of Juana in a straight line towards the north-west for no less than eight hundred thousand paces or eighty leagues, which led him to believe that it was a continent, since as far as the eye could reach, no signs of any limits to the island were perceptible.*

He decided to return, also because of the tumultuous sea, for the coast of Juana towards the north is very broken, and at that winter season, the north winds were dangerous to his ships. Laying his course eastwards, he held towards an island which he believed to be the island of **Ophir***; examination of the maps, however, shows that it was the Antilles and neighboring islands. He named this island Hispaniola.*

Having decided to land, Columbus put in towards shore, when the largest of his ships struck a concealed rock and was wrecked. Fortunately the reef stood high in the water, which saved the crew from drowning; the other two boats quickly approached, and all the sailors were taken safely on board.

Columbus thus indicated to Martyr that he thought that he had found the kingdom of Ophir which King Solomon's fleet had found in ancient times. Columbus believed that Ophir might have been the source of Solomon's gold.

When Hernán Cortés first met Moctezuma, the ruler of the Aztec kingdom, Moctezuma made a speech that indicated he believed Cortés was the reincarnation of Quetzalcoatl, the founder of the Aztec people. According to their myth, that founding father had come from far away, stayed with their ancestors, giving them agriculture, astronomy, written language, and all other technology, and then had sailed away, promising to return some day. Cortés arrived, coincidentally, just when the legend said their founder would return. Moctezuma made the following speech to Cortés:

O our lord, be doubly welcomed on your arrival in this land; you have come to satisfy your curiosity about your altepetl [kingdom] of Mexico, you have come to sit on your seat of authority, which I have kept a while for you, where I have been in charge for you, for your agents the rulers: Itzcoatzin, the elder Moctezuma, Axayacatl, Ticocic, and Ahuitzotl. They have gone, who for a very short time came to be in charge for you, to govern the altepetl of Mexico. It is after them that your poor vassal came. Will they come back to the place of their absence? If only one of them could see and behold what has now happened in my time, what I now see after our lords are gone. For I am not just dreaming, not just sleepwalking, not just seeing it in my sleep. I am not dreaming that I have seen you, have looked upon your face. For a time I have been concerned, looking toward the mysterious place from which you have come, among clouds and mist. It is so that the rulers on departing said that you would come in order to acquaint yourself with your altepetl and sit upon your seat of authority. And now it has come true, you have come. Be doubly welcome, enter the land, go to enjoy your palace, rest your body. May our lords be arrived in the land. Florentine Codex

Francisco Lopez de Gomara, sixteenth-century Spanish historian, wrote that the people of Cozumel "and other places … honored the cross." The Spanish took this to indicate that Christians had influenced the people of Mexico before Cortés conquered them. That, coupled with the Madoc legend and the speech by Moctezuma, put the Spaniards on the lookout for other signs of Madoc's presence in the Americas.

Finally, Madoc biographer Dana Olson reports that on a map by Diego Ribero dated 1519, in a collection in Seville, he has found this inscription, "Tierra de los Gales," which he translates as "Land of the Welsh." He says that this inscription accompanies a line pointing to modern-day Mobile Bay on the Gulf of Mexico. Madoc proponents most often point to that location as the point of entry of Madoc into the North American continent.

With that background, here is Madoc's story. On his first voyage to America, Madoc sailed with one or more ships from Wales about 1169. Whether he followed the tried and true northern route of the Vikings to Vinland the Good and then explored the continent or took the southerly route later followed by Christopher Columbus, we do not know. One

argument in favor of the southern route to the Americas is Madoc's previous travels to Spain and the Mediterranean. From his voyage there, he would have learned of Phoenician voyages down the west coast of Africa and possibly have known about the prevailing winds at the latitude of the Canaries favoring a crossing there.

Columbus's notation on his chart about Welsh waters in the West Indies would indicate that Madoc followed the southern route. Further, from Columbus's second voyage we learn that he found several wrecked ships of antiquity near Guadeloupe. The nationality of the ships could not be determined, but they clearly did not look like the work of Indians.

According to the Welsh literature, Madoc returned from America to Wales prior to 1170. He had left some people in the New World and had returned to recruit and transport a large number of people for his new colony. The Welsh stories indicate that Madoc's colonists encountered hostile indigenous people with whom they fought, and in the process moved up the river network that connects with Mobile Bay.

A record from Lundy Island off the coast of Wales indicates that Madoc sailed again from Wales with at least two ships in 1170, and those ships failed to return to Wales by 1171 at which time they were listed as missing at sea.

Madoc sailed on *Gwenan Gorn*. His brother, Riryd, sailed on *Pedr Sant*. A seventeenth-century scholar added two more names to Madoc's manifest: Edwal and Enion. They supposedly had a fleet of ten ships, with seven of them filled with passengers. These ships could easily have carried several hundred passengers.

With Madoc's links to both Wales and Ireland, we can assume that he recruited colonists in both countries. Riryd was Lord of Clochran in Ireland. The members of this expedition probably included people of Viking and Celtic ancestry, thus some with dark hair and eyes and others with fair hair and blue or grey eyes.

Once in America, Madoc's settlers went up the Alabama River to the Coosa River near Montgomery, Alabama, then crossed over to the Tennessee River near Chattanooga, Tennessee. They followed the Tennessee River to its confluence with the Ohio River, at Paducah, Kentucky. Once on the Ohio, they journeyed down river to the Mississippi River near Cairo, Illinois. Traveling up the Mississippi River, Madoc's settlers took the Missouri River near Oldenburg, Missouri. Heading west along the Missouri, they ended their journey just west of modern-day Bismarck, North Dakota, where the Heart River joins the Missouri.

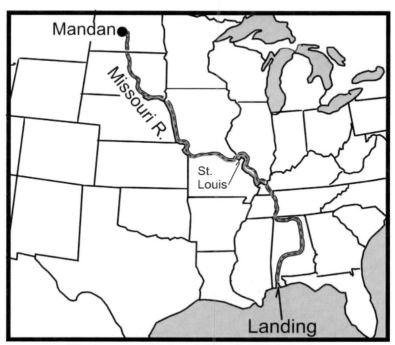

The journey of Prince Madoc's Welsh settlers
From Mobile Bay, Alabama to Bismarck, North Dakota

This journey covered several thousand miles and probably spanned many generations. Along the way, the Welsh settlers interacted with the Native Americans—not always in friendly ways. They built a series of stone forts along their route through Alabama, Georgia, Tennessee, Kentucky and along the Ohio River. Remnants of those forts still exist and authorities including the Park Service speculate that non-Indians built those constructions in stone. The following letter from the early nineteenth century when the westward expansion of the English colonies began sheds some light on the story of Madoc's settlers' long journey through Indian territories:

To Amos Stoddard

I shall with pleasure, give you the information required, so far as my memory will now serve me, and the help of a memorandum I hastily took on the subject, of a nation of people called the Welsh Indians. In the year 1782, I was on a campaign against the Cherokees, and during my route, discovered traces of very ancient fortifications. Some time after the expedition, I had occasion to enter into a negotiation with the Cherokee Chiefs, for the purpose of exchanging prisoners.

After the exchange had been settled, I took an opportunity of enquiring of a venerable old chief, named Oconostoto, (then, and for nearly sixty years had been, a ruling chief of the Cherokee nation,) if he could inform me of the people that had left such signs of fortifications in their country and particularly the one on the bank of the Highwassee river?

The old warrior briefly answered me as follows: It is handed down by our forefather, that the works were made by white people, who had formerly inhabited the country, while the

Cherokees lived low down in the country, now called South Carolina, and that a war existed between the two nations for many years. At length, it was discovered, that the whites were making a number of large boats, which induced the Cherokees to suppose, that they intended to descend the river.

They then collected their whole band of warriors, and took the shortest and most convenient route to the muscle shoals in order to intercept them down the river. In a few days, the boats hove in sight, and a warm combat ensued, with various success for several days. At length the whites proposed to the Indians, that if they would exchange prisoners, and cease hostilities, they would leave the country, and never more return; which was acceded to, and, after the exchange, parted in friendship. The whites then descended the Tennessee to the Ohio, and then down to the big river, (Mississippi) then up it to the muddy river, (Missouri) then up that river to a very great distance. They are now on some of its branches; But they are no longer a white people; they are now all become Indians; and look like the other red people of the country.

I then asked him, if he had ever heard any of his ancestors say what nation of people those white people belonged to? He answered; "I have heard my grandfather and other old people say, that they were a people called, Welsh; that they had crossed the great water, and landed near the mouth of Alabama river, and were finally driven to the heads of its water, and even to Highwassee river, by the Mexican Indians, who had been driven out to their own country by the Spaniards.

Many years past I happened in company with a Frenchman, who lived with the Cherokees, and had been a great explorer of the country west of the Mississippi. He informed me, "that he had been high up the Missouri, and traded several months with the Welsh tribe; that they spoke much of the Welsh dialect, and although their customs were savage and wild, yet many of them, particularly the females were very fair and white, and frequently told him, they had sprung from a white nation of people; also stated they had yet some small scraps of books remaining among them, but in such tattered and destructive order, that nothing intelligible remained." He observed that their settlement was in a very obscure part of the Missouri, surrounded with innumerable lofty mountains. The Frenchman's name has escaped my memory, but I believe it was something like Duroque.

In my conversation with the old chief Oconostoto, he informed me, that an old woman in his nation named Peg, had some part of an old book given her by an Indian living high up the Missouri, and thought he was one of the Welsh tribe. Unfortunately before I had an opportunity of seeing the book, the old woman's house and its contents were consumed by fire. I have conversed with several persons, who saw and examined the book, but it was so worn and disfigured, that nothing intelligible remained; neither did any one of them understand any language but their own, and even that, very imperfectly.

John Sevier, Knoxville, Tennessee, October 9th, 1810

As this letter portrays, the long journey of the Welsh people to find a safe haven in the New World finally led them to modern-day North Dakota. By then, they had suffered great losses and had been partially assimilated by Native Americans who were friendly to them or whom they captured in battle. The assimilation of Madoc's settlers' descendants produced a mélange of Irish, Welsh, Norse, and American

Indian genetic characteristics. Those people of this mixing of cultures had the name Mandan by the time Canadian and later American explorers encountered them for the first time.

Early visitors to the Mandan villages reported that their people looked like no other Indians they had seen. A number of the Mandan had light skin, light colored hair, blue or grey eyes, and European facial features. Although those people were a minority among the people of the villages, they comprised a significant percentage—estimated by one visitor to be about twenty percent of the tribe.

Visitors noted other aspects of the Mandan that appeared foreign among all the other Indian tribes. They laid their villages out on a rectilinear pattern of paths, their houses were distinctly different from the other Indians, and they had a most unusual form of watercraft. Where other Indians used log or bark canoes, the Mandan used "bull boats." The bull boats were round in shape like a basin, framed of willow or other flexible boughs and covered with animal skin.

A Mandan woman in one of their unusual "Bull Boats"

A Canadian explorer, Pierre Gaultier de Varennes, Sieur (Lord) de Vérendrye, first "discovered" the Mandan in 1738—he had gone looking for a rumored tribe of White Indians, an indication of how widespread the story of White or Welsh Indians was. The Spanish looked for them in their explorations of North America, the American pioneers looked for them, and even the French Canadians had heard about these strange people.

Vérendrye found the Mandan at their villages living near the Arikara, Pawnee, Sioux, and other Indian tribes. He reported that they lived in six fortified villages along the Missouri River. Here is Vérendrye's description of one Mandan village and the people he found there.

After the departure, M. de Lamarque and I took a walk to examine the extent of their fortifications. I gave orders to count the cabins, and we found that there were about one hundred and thirty. All the streets, squares and cabins are uniform in appearance; often our Frenchmen would lose their way in going about. They keep the streets and open spaces very clean; the ramparts are smooth and wide; the palisade is supported on cross pieces mortised into the posts fifteen feet apart with a lining. For this purpose they use green hides fastened only at the top in places where they are needed. As to the bastions, there are four of them at each curtain well flanked. The fort is built on an elevation in mid-prairie with a ditch over fifteen feet deep and from fifteen to eighteen wide. Entrance to the fort can only be obtained by steps or pieces of wood which they remove when threatened by the enemy. If all their forts are similar you may say that they are impregnable to savages.

This tribe is of mixed blood, white and black. The women are rather handsome, particularly the light-colored ones; they have an abundance of fair hair. The whole tribe, men and women, is very industrious. Their dwellings are large and spacious, divided into several apartments by wide planks. Nothing is lying about: all their belongings are placed in large bags hung on posts; their beds are made in the form of tombs [compartments] and are surrounded by skins. They all go to bed naked, both men and women. The men go naked all the time, being covered only by a buffalo robe. Many of the women go naked like the men, with this difference, that they wear a small loin-cloth about a hand wide and a foot long sewed to a girdle in front only. All the women wear this kind of protection even when they wear a petticoat, so that they are not embarrassed when they sit down and do not have to keep the thighs closed like other Indian women. Some wear a kind of jacket of very soft buckskin.

Their fort is very well provided with cellars, where they store all they have in the way of grains, meat, fat, dressed skins and bearskins. They have a great stock of these things, which form the money of the country. The more they have the richer they consider themselves. ... The men are big and tall, very active and, for the most part, good-looking, fine physiognomies, and affable. The women generally have not a savage cast of features.

Vérendrye thus described the Mandan as an advanced culture among the Plains Indians in the early eighteenth century. He found them a mixture of white and Indian people. That would have been expected of people descended from Native Americans and some infusion of people from Europe nearly five hundred years before. Whether the

Mandan represented a blending of Madoc's Celtic settlers among indigenous tribes or, as some have argued, Norse settlers and Indians, we cannot conclusively say. But from this earliest Canadian explorer, it seems possible that the Mandan represented a mélange of European and Native American cultures.

At the time of Vérendrye's visit, the Mandan probably numbered in the thousands. Six fortified villages with one hundred and thirty or so houses would have held about five or six thousand people. They would receive additional European and American visitors, including Lewis and Clark, in the next one hundred years. Most of those visitors would report finding the same mix of Mandan people with European features and American Indian features.

In 1841, artist George Catlin wrote, "There are a great many of these people whose complexions appear as light as half-breeds; and amongst the women particularly there are many whose skins are almost white. ...The diversity in the color of hair is equally as great as that in the complexion; for in a numerous group of these people ... there may be seen every shade and color of hair that can be seen in our own country, with the exception of red or auburn."

Catlin, who had lived with the Mandan for nearly a year in 1832-1833, also observed the high degree of sophistication of the Mandan in comparison to the numerous other tribes he lived with and portrayed in his paintings. He wrote that they "... claimed to be descended from a white man who came in a big canoe ...." The Mandan had various religious fragments including a story of the virgin birth of a savior, a flood myth very similar to the story of Noah. Other Indians had flood myths, but the Mandan story was uncharacteristically close to the Biblical story, as if they had in the distant path been

An 1849 Portrait of George Catlin by William Fisk

taught the Bible stories and, over the succeeding centuries, the stories had become synthesized with Indian beliefs, yet retained their Biblical fundamentals.

Catlin also observed the most unusual style of watercraft that the Mandan used on the Missouri River. The boat they used was a coracle—built of flexible boughs in the same manner as the Celtic craft and covered with buffalo skin. And the paddle the Mandan used was identical to that used to this day in parts of Wales. The upper end of the shaft had a rounded grip or claw carved into it.

Catlin believed the Mandan represented the remnants of the Welsh brought by Madoc assimilated into some ancient Indian tribe. He found similarity in some of their words to Welsh words. Linguists today find no such similarity; but that cannot be surprising when we know what happened to the Mandan after contact with nineteenth-century explorers.

A year after Catlin left the Mandan, a German named A. P. Maximilian, Prince of Wied, studied the Mandan. He wrote about the same peculiar characteristics reported by Vérendrye and Catlin. The Mandan were "almost white." Their fortified villages bore no resemblance to the other Plains Indians villages. They had religious sagas, he reported, that could have come directly from the Bible including stories of Noah's Ark, the flood, and the story of Samson.

Not long after Catlin and Maximilian studied the Mandan, a boat of traders visited their locale. Some of the Mandan boarded the boat and came away with the smallpox virus. It spread quickly to their villages with devastating results. By 1836, there were about 1,800 Mandan. By 1838, their number had dropped to about 125. In 1971, thirty full-blooded Mandan existed.

The Mandan, the Arikara, and the Hidatsa banded together as their numbers dwindled due to disease and depredations from neighboring hostile tribes. By the end of the American Civil War, the three combined tribes lived at the Fort Berthold Indian Reservation in North Dakota. Today, only one Mandan elder can speak the old language. The language that Catlin and others said contained Welsh words now bears no resemblance to Welsh. Modern linguists characterize Mandan as a Siouan dialect. But what was it really two hundred to three hundred years ago when Catlin and others likened it to Welsh? We will never know.

Other accounts of Welsh Indians include a report by Daniel Boone of blue-eyed Indians in Kentucky and Tennessee, which fits the migration pattern of Madoc's settlers as recounted by the Cherokee. And then there's Reverend Morgan Jones's strange tale. Reverend Jones, a Welsh speaker, had been to the Carolinas and was returning to Virginia through the back country in the 1680s. On that trip, Indians of the Doeg tribe captured Jones and planned to execute him. In his anguish, he spoke in Welsh, these words given in English, "Have I escaped so many dangers and must now be knocked on the head like a dog!" One of the Indians overheard him and began to speak to him in Welsh. The Doeg allowed Jones to live with them for several months and then he returned to Virginia. In earlier times the Doeg occupied the Virginia side of the Potomac River. At least one other early explorer connected the Doeg to the Welsh. An interesting linguistic coincidence is that in Welsh, Madoc is pronounced Madog.

This story of Madoc's settlers in America appears to have no end, and the Internet keeps it alive today. While no conclusive proof of Madoc's people making it to America has been discovered to date, many people for hundreds of years have believed that the Welsh beat Christopher Columbus to America by three hundred and twenty-two years.

Chapter 10
Estotiland and Drogio

In 1371, a storm blew fishermen from the Orkney Isles a thousand miles or more across the western sea to a large island called Estotiland according to one of the survivors. Some modern-day researchers think Estotiland was Newfoundland. One of the fishermen reported that he lived among the people of Estotiland for five years. He said they traded with Greenland. The people of Estotiland were civilized and treated the fishermen well. The Estotilanders possessed books written in Latin.

The fishermen left Estotiland and traveled south to a country called Drogio. Drogio extended a great distance and they considered it a new world—that is a continent. Dense forests covered this new land, and the fishermen encountered hostile people living there. All but one of the fishermen died at the hands of the people living along the cost of Drogio, and the sole survivor lived among them thirteen years before he made his escape back to Estotiland.

Finally, the fisherman built a boat at Estotiland and sailed back to the Orkney Isles to tell his tale to Sir Henry Sinclair, the Earl of Orkney. Sir Henry was the son of Sir William Sinclair, Earl of Rosslyn, and Isobel of Strathearn. When Henry came of age, King Haakon VI of Norway conferred on him the title Earl of Orkney. Sir Henry Sinclair fought to assert his control, on behalf of King Haakon, over the Shetlands and Faroes. In his attempt to subdue those islands, Sir Henry had in his service two Venetian seafarers named

Nicolò and Antonio Zeno. Nicolò served as Sinclair's pilot, and later Antonio arrived and entered into Sinclair's service.

Nicolò set off on a voyage of discovery to Greenland, but found the climate not to his liking. He returned to the Orkney Isles where he died. Then Antonio accompanied the Earl on a voyage to investigate the territory of Estotiland and Drogio.

Estotiland and Drogio shown on a map of the Atlantic in 1570

This entire story of Estotiland, Drogio, the brothers Zeno, and the Earl of Sinclair comes down to us in a curious and highly problematic way. First, the Zeno brothers are real historical figures, although much of their life is rather ill-defined in reliable documents. Likewise, Sir Henry Sinclair, the Earl of Orkney existed, although his history also lacks details.

135

The source of the tale is a book titled *Dello scoprimento dell' isole Frislanda, Eslanda, Engrouelanda, Estotilanda e Icaria fatto sotto il Polo artico da' due fratelli Zeni, M. Nicolo il K. e M. Antonio.* The book contains transcripts of the Zeno brothers' letters totaling about seven thousand words telling of their adventures in the North Atlantic during the fourteenth century. The book was accompanied by a map of the North Atlantic identifying the peculiarly named locations that appear in the narrative. Another Nicolò Zeno, descendant of the subjects of this story, published the book, which appeared in print in Venice in 1558—nearly two hundred years after the events in the narrative.

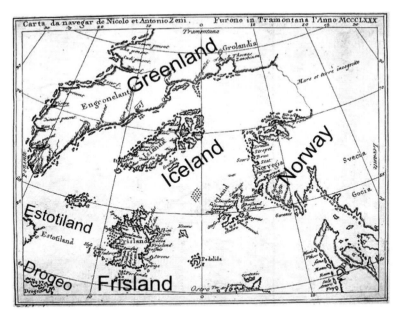

A 1793 copy of the Zeno Map of 1558

The first of several problems with the narrative from the sixteenth century Zeno descendant is the map of the North Atlantic and the names of important locales in the story of the Zeno brothers and Sir Henry Sinclair. The sixteenth-century book refers to the man the Zeno brothers served as Zichmni. That name is a far cry from Sinclair, although it may bear some resemblance to Orkney. The narrative also refers to the islands owned by Zichmni as Porlanda, located off the south coast of Frislanda. Other names on the map and in the narrative bear no resemblance to the Orkney Isles, the Shetlands, or the Faroes.

So it seems reasonable to ask how the Zeno brothers came to be connected to the Earl of Orkney, Sir Henry Sinclair. John Reinhold Forster, a travel writer, made that connection in 1780. He suggested that Zichmni was Henry Sinclair. Since no such island as Frislanda exists in the North Atlantic—supposedly an island larger than Ireland—Forster speculated that Frislanda had sunk beneath the waves after an earthquake like the lost civilization of Atlantis. Thus began the legend of Sir Henry Sinclair's exploration of Estotiland.

A Sinclair genealogy of the first Sinclair Earl of Orkney written within fifty years of his death makes no mention of Sir Henry being a maritime explorer. So this tale seems to have no merit. Also, modern research in the archives of Venice discloses that Nicolò Zeno's occupation from 1380 until his death circa 1400 left no time for his mythical adventures in the North Atlantic with Sir Henry Sinclair. To the contrary, Nicolò Zeno commanded a squadron of Venetian galleys, served as Governor of Corone and Modone in Greece, and later served as a councilor to the Doge of

Venice until he stood trial for embezzlement in 1396. After paying a fine of 200 gold ducats, he apparently lived out his few remaining years in Venice. Nicolò Zeno could not have sailed the North Atlantic with Sir Henry Sinclair or with someone named Zichmni between 1380 and 1400.

However, the legend of Sir Henry Sinclair exploring America has continued throughout nearly two hundred thirty years. Ardent supporters of this story have come up with a number of arguments to bolster the idea that Henry Sinclair actually came to America—to Nova Scotia, in fact, landing on Trinity Sunday, June 2, 1398. Their arguments do little to eliminate all the contradictions between the Zeno narrative and map with what was known of the North Atlantic in the fourteenth century or even what we know today. Instead, they take it as proven that Zichmni was Sinclair, and slog on from there with a link between Sir Henry Sinclair and a Micmac Indian legend as well as a purported "fourteenth century cannon" found off Cape Breton Island as indicative of the Zeno presence there.

Let's take the cannon first. The cannon at Fortress Louisbourg turns out to be a fairly common swivel gun with banded barrel reinforcement. Heidi Moses, the Archaeology Collections Manager at the fort, gave me the following account of this crucial physical link between America and the Zeno brothers in the fourteenth century:

It [the cannon or petrieroe] *was found along the north shore of Louisbourg harbour (either in the mud or brought up by a ship's anchor) in the 1840s and given to the Louisbourg Museum in 1936 by Mrs. George Burchell whose husband, Captain George Burchell, had purchased it ca. 1880. We have*

*been advised by Robert Smith, Head of Conservation, Royal
Armouries, London, that the cannon (which may possibly be
Portuguese in origin) does not date before the middle of the 16th
century and was …still being used into the late 1660s. As a
matter of fact, guns of this nature were used in Louisbourg, by
the French, in the 1740s.*

So much for the "fourteenth century Venetian cannon."

Now to the Indian legend. The Micmac have stories of
Glooscap, their creator-god, whom some Henry Sinclair
enthusiasts assert resembles Sir Henry in the guise of a
European explorer landing among the ancestors of the
Micmac in fourteenth-century Nova Scotia. Supposedly,
Glooscap was a white man who came from the east and
brought all sorts of civilizing aspects to the native population.

One article on this subject even asserts that Henry
Sinclair taught the Micmac how to play a Scottish hockey
stick-and-ball game called "Shinny." The Micmac were
observed playing this Scottish game by British soldiers who
founded Halifax about 1749. Likewise, early contact with the
Micmac in the fifteenth century supposedly revealed that they
had knowledge of Christianity and could speak, in a limited
way, a number of European languages.

Taking the idea of knowledge of Christianity and
European languages first, that should not seem surprising
given the much earlier and well-established contact in the
northeast region of America by Norse and perhaps Irish
explorers including Scandinavian Christians and possibly Irish
monks. We don't need Sir Henry Sinclair to bring that
knowledge to the Indians of North America four or more
centuries later.

As to the comparisons of Henry Sinclair and Glooscap, they really strain credibility. Glooscap, at least according to the modern version of this Indian god, was huge in size—able to form river valleys with his bare hands. Glooscap turned himself into a giant beaver and formed islands by slapping his immense tail against the sea with such force that the sediments on the sea bottom rose up above the sea. Sir Henry Sinclair must have been an incredible Scotsman to achieve these feats. Those who compare Sinclair to Glooscap take a fabulous tale of an adventuring Scot and equate him to an even more fabulous god-figure of Indian mythology. One gives no credence to the other, since both tales are incredible.

Other Sinclair proponents add details intended to establish that Henry Sinclair not only visited Nova Scotia, but lived there for a time. They point to a faintly carved stone in Westford, Massachusetts, as the burial effigy of Sir James Gunn, a Templar Knight who supposedly sailed to America with Henry Sinclair. According to this recently concocted legend, Gunn died in America and his companions carved the outline of a Templar Knight complete with long sword and coat of arms into a convenient boulder. The area where the boulder rests is far from the sea, and in the fourteenth century, the boulder was probably under about four feet of soil in a dense forest. The area, now the city of Westford, experienced significant erosion after the forest was cleared, and eventually the boulder appeared due to those natural forces.

The preceding will hopefully dismiss the story of Sir Henry Sinclair coming to Nova Scotia, or Massachusetts, or Rhode Island, as unsupportable mythology—mythology of rather recent creation at that.

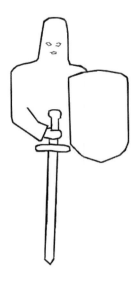

The Westford Knight carving
As seen by Sir Henry Sinclair advocates

Chapter 11
Back to Fu Sang

On March 5, 1421, fishermen off the coast of China saw an incredible sight. More than one hundred huge, ocean-going junks sailed out into the Yellow Sea with colorful banners streaming from their mast tops, born on a southerly route by a wind from the northeast. These ships, nearly five hundred feet long, with a beam of one hundred eighty feet, carried two thousand tons of cargo and passengers. They carried huge expanses of red silk sails on nine masts and had equally massive rudders on posts thirty-six-feet high. By comparison, European ships of the day barely exceeded in length the height of the Chinese junks' rudder posts.

Chinese ship of the 15th century

Accompanying these massive ships, ninety-foot-long merchant ships carried additional provisions and supplies as well as trade goods for a voyage anticipated to last more than one year. Beyond that second echelon of ships, heavily-armed warships with mounted cannon and other deadly weapons protected the armada from pirates. In total, several hundred ships comprised Emperor Zhu Di's fleet under the command of his most trusted Admiral Zheng He. As many as 27,000 people sailed with the admiral.

Zheng He was a Muslim eunuch—originally called Ma Sanbao—who came from the Yunnan province that, at the time of his birth in 1371, was the last land to be brought under the Ming Dynasty. His distant ancestors came from Uzbekistan. In 1381, Ming raiders captured eleven-year-old Ma and castrated him. They took him to the Ming imperial court where he served the Yongle emperor, Zhu Di. Ma studied at the imperial college of Nanjing Taixue and somehow caught the eye of the emperor. In time, he rose to prominence, advising the emperor and receiving the honorary name of Zheng He. Zheng He led seven voyages from China to Southeast Asia, India, the Persian Gulf, and Eastern Africa—at least as far as modern-day Kenya—between 1405 and 1433, each lasting about two years. In 1433, Zheng He died at sea off Calcutta, returning from his seventh voyage.

The Chinese armada of 1421 comprised four of the five Chinese fleets. Its mission was twofold: to return ambassadors to their home countries and to spread the word throughout the world that Zhu Di ruled over the great Chinese empire. Ambassadors from Persia, India, Southeast Asia and Africa had come to China as guests aboard ships during previous voyages of Zheng He, and now sailed home in opulence at the emperor's expense.

Ming Emperor Zhu Di

Zheng He had orders to explore all parts of the world and present tokens of Zhu Di's realm to every civilization he encountered. His earlier voyages had taken him at least as far as East Africa, and one souvenir he brought to the emperor was a giraffe—thought of by the Chinese as a mythical beast they called the qilin. His last voyage went at least as far. On a tablet engraved to commemorate Zheng He's voyages, he left this enigmatic statement:

We have traversed more than 100,000 li [30,000 miles]
of immense water spaces and have beheld in the ocean huge

waves like mountains rising in the sky, and we have set eyes on barbarian regions far away hidden in a blue transparency of light vapors, while our sails, loftily unfurled like clouds day and night, continued their course [as rapidly] *as a star, traversing those savage waves as if we were treading a public thoroughfare...*

A giraffe, the Chinese mythical Qilin brought from Africa by Admiral Zheng He for Emperor Zhu Di

Aleck Loker

In 1459, Fra Mauro, a Venetian cartographer, produced a map with what appears to some scholars to be a Chinese junk sailing into the Atlantic Ocean. The map bears a notation that indicates the junk originated in India and traveled 2,000 miles. The route taken by Zheng He's fleet and the farthest extent of their voyage is unknown; however, tantalizing clues from around the world give an indication that they may have reached North America.

About 1420 a Junk from India

Detail from the Fra Mauro Map
North is toward the bottom and the land shown is the south coast of Africa. The ship is sailing toward the Atlantic Ocean.
The highlighted Italian text says "About 1420 a junk from India…"

The most recent proponent of this theory, Gavin Menzies, caught the public's imagination in 2002 with his publication of *1421: The year China Discovered America*. Orthodox historians scoff at his theory and dismiss it as the imagination of an amateur.

Menzies arrived at his theory by examining maps in Italian, Portuguese and Spanish possession at the end of the fifteenth century. Menzies believed that those maps showed details of the West Indies that western European states could not have obtained from their own explorations. Menzies postulates that those maps must have come from or been derived from Chinese maps of the world produced at the time of Zheng He, if not many years before.

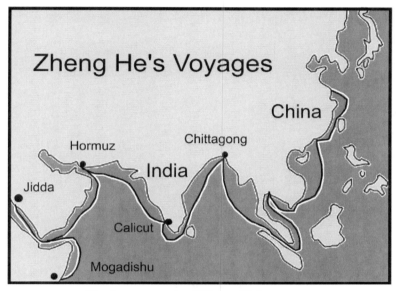

The known route of Zheng He's voyages

According to Menzies' scenario, Zheng He's fleet sailed to the Indian subcontinent, then down the east coast of Africa. Once at the southern tip of Africa, the fleet broke into its constituent parts and each took a different route of exploration. One section, according to Menzies, sailed to the Americas, leaving traces of Chinese culture at their various landfalls. As in any operation of this scale, some ships would have been lost at sea, others would have wrecked on the uncharted coasts, and Chinese men and materials would thus be left behind in the New World.

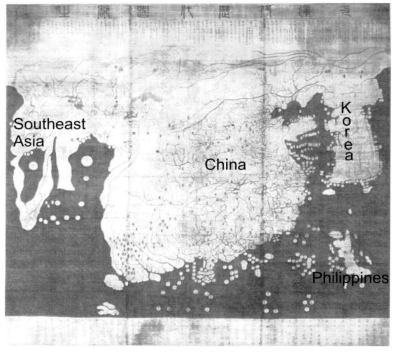

Kangnido Map of 1402
Believed to have been used by Admiral Zheng He

Menzies identified many signs of Chinese contact in the Americas. From Chapter 4 we know that the Chinese may have come to America a number of times well before 1421, including as early as the 2200 BCE geographic exploration for Emperor Shun, and the sixth-century CE pilgrimage of Buddhist monk Hui Shan. Because those much earlier contacts between China and the Americas could account for some of Menzies' evidence, we will focus on a few clues found in North America that point to contact by the Chinese during the reign of Zhu Di or other Ming dynasty rulers. For the other clues to Chinese contact in America, Australia, and other far flung lands, Menzies' book and website will provide all the fascinating details.

In 1994, R. W. Shinnick used a metal detector to search a churchyard near Ashville, North Carolina, for old coins and historical artifacts. He found pennies of fairly recent vintage and as he continued his search, he found older pennies (Indian Head pennies) at a greater depth. Then, at a depth of four inches, he found a circular brass or bronze disk with a diameter of about 2.75 inches. The disc is blank on the back and has a raised square centered on the front. The square area contains Chinese characters.

Shinnick collects coins. He relegated the strange disc to a drawer at home where he put mysterious items or bits of junk that he didn't want to discard. The disc lay in his drawer for a number of years. Then in 2006, he photographed the disc and posted images of it on the Internet, seeking a translation of the Chinese characters and interest in the item. Dr. S. L. Lee of Columbus, Ohio, contacted Shinnick and purchased the disc.

The message on the disc reads, "Authorized and awarded by Xuande of Great Ming." Lee recognized the significance of this disc. Although he is careful to say that he has reached no conclusion regarding the disc's authenticity, he reports that the disc's composition is a form of brass characteristic of the period of transition between bronze and brass during the time of the Ming emperors. Modern brass has a different ratio of component metals.

There is a problem attributing this disc to the voyage of Zheng He in 1421. The emperor during the Xuande period was Zhu Zhanji and the date would be 1426 to 1435. So, if this disc is authentic, it would seem that Menzies has Zheng He sailing to America too early or perhaps Zheng He made multiple voyages to America. However, the historical record seems to preclude any voyage by Zheng He after the sixth voyage of 1421/2 until his seventh voyage of 1430 to 1433. Zheng He died returning from this last voyage of exploration and ambassadorial duties. There would be no further voyages as future Ming emperors turned inward and forbade trade with the far flung nations.

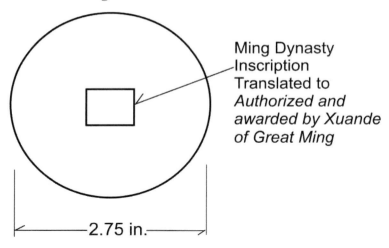

Ming era brass presentation disk found by R. W. Shinnick

Lee observes that the disc was found in an area occupied by the Cherokee Indians at the time of the Revolutionary War. He speculates that they could have possessed the disc and lost it at the location near Ashville. Lee says that the

Ming emperors commissioned such discs for presentation by their ambassadors to foreign nations. Thus, this disc could represent contact between Chinese explorers of the fifteenth century and the Native Americans of the Carolinas.

He adds to this discovery of the disc that the Catawba tribe that lived along the Carolina coast were noted for their pottery, which he says compared in form to "bronze censers made in the Xuan De era." Although the Catawba did not make porcelain pottery, they had knowledge of how to produce the white clay from stones—the basis for the Chinese porcelain industry. They produced a type of stoneware instead of the more delicate, high-fired porcelain. So Lee sees possible evidence of Chinese contact during the Ming period with the Native American tribes of the mid-Atlantic region. He also observes that the Catawba word for pottery clay was unaker—remarkably similar to the uk-na-ke in Ming era Chinese.

On the Pacific coast, another Ming Dynasty artifact turned up in the woods of Northern California fifty years ago. Orval Stokes found what he thought was an automobile hubcap sticking up out of the forest floor near Susanville, California. He pulled the object out of the ground and it seemed too heavy to be a hubcap. Like the metal-detectorist in North Carolina, Mr. Stokes took the object home and then forgot about it for a few years.

When Mr. Stokes re-examined the object after cleaning it, he saw that it was a plate made of bronze or brass and, like the disc in North Carolina, had a series of what appeared to him to be Chinese characters in the center of the plate. Then Mr. Stokes lost interest in the artifact again.

Forty years later, a Chinese couple moved into Mr. Stokes' neighborhood, and he remembered the brass plate. When the Chinese couple examined it, they said it looked like a Ming Dynasty plate. Mr. Stokes turned the plate over to Yixian Xu, a history professor at Idaho State University, who translated the inscription as, "Made in the reign of Xuan De of the Ming Dynasty."

This second Chinese artifact dating to the Ming Dynasty found on the opposite side of North America gives additional credence to the theory of Chinese contact in the Americas about seventy years before Christopher Columbus's first voyage of discovery.

Archaeologists usually say these finds that amateurs report are unconvincing. They dismiss them as either intentional hoaxes or merely discarded collectibles brought back to America by modern-era travelers. Archaeologists have used that same argument to dismiss the evidence of various items of clearly human design attributed to Libyan, Irish, Phoenician, Norse, and Chinese visitors hundreds to thousands of years ago.

The idea that these two examples of Chinese contact with the Americas are hoaxes seems implausible. Both of the people involved found the artifacts in a context that appears genuine; in the North Carolina case, buried in the ground in an undisturbed context; and in the California case, in a forest far from non-Native American habitation. Both of the finders paid no particular attention to the finds for a long period of time and made no attempt to capitalize on them in terms of seeking publicity or even significant monetary reward. In both cases, the finders had no idea of the significance of their finds until experts in the field determined what they had found and assessed the importance of the artifacts. It seems unlikely either Mr. Shinnick or Mr. Stokes engaged in hoaxes.

As to the idea that modern-day collectors absentmindedly discarded these two Ming Dynasty artifacts, that also makes no sense. In North Carolina, the artifact was four inches deep in undisturbed soil. The owner would have had to have lost it hundreds of years before Mr. Shinnick found it. What would an early colonial pioneer in the west of North Carolina have been doing with a Ming Dynasty presentation disc? It seems unlikely that the disc was intentionally discarded. Dr. Lee's theory of the disc being in the possession of Native American's makes more sense.

The Ming artifact found in a forest in California could have been hidden there by robbers, but probably not unintentionally lost, or intentionally discarded there. Who goes walking in the woods with a Ming plate? If burglars stashed the plate there with the intention of returning for it later, they left it in an unusual position, standing on edge half out of the soil. Again, this scenario seems rather implausible.

You seldom hear of anyone stumbling onto an important artifact of English origin in an out-of-the-way place—with the exception of military remains found at known battlefield sites by metal-detectorists. Yet English artifacts dating back four hundred years would seem to be more likely to be accidentally found by amateurs. Instead, those sorts of artifacts turn up in professional archaeological digs at targeted sites. Why would collectors be so careless with more ancient remnants of Libyan, Norse, Irish, Chinese, or Phoenician artifacts? I doubt either of the Ming Dynasty artifacts described above was brought to America by European colonists or American tourists during the last six hundred years.

On the west coast, a much larger Chinese artifact, one that a careless collector did not discard, may tie fifteenth-century Chinese voyagers to America. About two hundred miles up the Sacramento River near Glenn, California, rumors of a Chinese junk buried in the sand brought Dr. John Furry, who operates the Museum of Northern California, to investigate this wreck site. In 1982 when he located it, the wreck could only be detected by magnetometer readings indicating a relatively large mass under the sand. Furry had borings made down to the mass and extracted bits of wood. The wood carbon dated to about 1410, putting its harvesting near the date of Zheng He's fleet. According to Menzies, the wood, later analyzed in China, proved to be of a species unique to China. Please note that this supposed Chinese junk lies under about forty feet of sand and gravel, has not been excavated, and people have known about it since the 1930s.

As with all of Menzies' claims, the Chinese junk in the Sacramento River may prove to have a more mundane explanation. Some of his other examples of Chinese contact in America now seem to have other explanations. For example, Menzies cited a find on the Oregon coast of an old wooden pulley block and beeswax that he said had a Chinese provenance perhaps dating to the fifteenth century. Menzies had a theory that the Chinese used wax to desalinate sea water. Further analysis has disclosed that the beeswax and the pulley date much too late to tie to Zheng He's fleet—1595 for the pulley and 1500 to 1650 for the beeswax. The pulley now appears to have come from a Spanish galleon of the conquest period. Whether Menzies theory holds up remains to be seen, but the Chinese fleet under Zheng He clearly had the capability to make it to America, Australia, or anywhere else they set their course.

An historical fragment contained in the papers of the Virginia Company of London—sponsors of the Jamestown settlements of 1607 and later—presents one more tantalizing clue. A letter sent to the Company by the Governor and Treasurer at the Virginia Colony in March, 1621 contained the following information:

> ... *Furthermore they write that in a voyage made by Lieutenant Marmaduke Parkinson, and other English Gentlemen, up the River of Patomack they saw a China Boxe at one of the Kings houses where they were: Being demanded where he had it, made answer, That it was sent him from a King that dwelt in the West, over the great Hills, some tenne dayes journey, whose Countrey is near a great Sea, hee having the Boxe, from a people as he said, that came thither in ships, that weare cloaths, crooked swords, & somewhat like our men, dwelt in houses and were called Acamack-China: and he offered our people, that he would send his Brother along with them to that King, which offer the Governor purposed not to refuse; and the rather, by reason of the continued constant relations of all those Savages in VIRGINIA, of a Sea, and the way to it West, they affirming that the heads of all those seven goodly Rivers, (the least whereof is greater then the River of Thames, and navigable above an hundred and fifty miles, and not above sixe or eight miles one from another) which fall all into one great Bay, have the rising out of a ridge of hills,*

that runnes all along South and North; Whereby they doubt not but to find a safe, easie, and good passage to the South Sea, part by water, and part by land, esteeming it not above an hundred and fifty miles from the head of the Falls, where we are now planted; the Discovery whereof will bring forth a most rich trade to Cathay, China, Japan, and those other of the East Indies, to the inestimable benefit of this Kingdom.

Clearly, the English were deluded about the proximity of the South Sea or Pacific Ocean to the Potomac River. But the "china box" does raise interesting questions. Did the Indians of the upper Potomac get the box in trade from others who had received it as a gift from Chinese explorers? What did the box look like? Unfortunately, the box disappeared from the record. Whether it made it to England and ended up in some official's home or never made it to England we will never know.

Chapter 12
João Vaz Corte-Real and Sons

In the early fifteenth century, Portugal held sway over the Atlantic. Prince Henrique (Henry), the third child of King João (John) I of Portugal and his English wife, Philippa of Lancaster (daughter of John of Gaunt), came to see the advantages to Portugal in exploration of the west coast of Africa. Henrique had three goals in mind: locate the site of gold mines along that coast; eliminate the area as a haven for pirates that preyed on Portuguese shipping; and locate the mythical Christian kingdom of Prester John. Prince Henry the Navigator—as Henrique is called in English—developed a new ship design to replace the slower and more cumbersome craft then in use.

Fifteenth century Portuguese ships sailing to India

Portuguese mariners sailed in these small but fast caravels that had the capability to weather the Atlantic seas. When he became governor of the Order of Christ, which had succeeded and assumed control of the wealth of the Order of Knights Templar, Prince Henry had the fortune he needed to finance his dreams of Portuguese expansion. His first accession in 1419 was the re-conquest of the Canary Islands, purportedly first occupied by the Portuguese by 1346. Prince Henry went on to establish Portuguese control over slave markets in Guinea on the west coast of Africa.

Although the main emphasis in Portugal at this time focused on exploring along the African coast and eventually opening a trade route past the Cape of Good Hope to India, Portugal also began to push west into the Atlantic. By 1418, they took control of Madeira, and they reached the easternmost islands of the Azores in 1427. Within twenty-five years, Portuguese mariners had reached the western extent of the Azores and the islands became settled as Portuguese possessions.

Prester John

Prester or Prebyster John was a legendary Christian ruler of a kingdom isolated among the Muslims in Africa or perhaps in Asia. This medieval tale remained popular in Europe from the 1200s to the 1700s. Prester John descended from one of the Three Magi, ruled over an area that included Fountain of Youth and bordered Paradise.

This kingdom contained great wealth. Perhaps the most prevalent aspect of the legend had Prester John ruling over his kingdom in Ethiopia. At certain times, Europeans thought he ruled over India. Eventually, the Portuguese reached India and found no trace of Prester John.

One of the early settlers in the Azores, João Vaz Corte-Real received a grant of land on Terceira Island—the third island settled in the Azores—in recognition of his discovery of land the Portuguese called Terra Nova do Bacalhau (New Land of Codfish). Corte-Real received this land grant in 1474. Presumably his discovery of the New Land of Codfish occurred no more than a year of so before the land grant in the Azores. Maps of the period one hundred years later clearly identify this land as modern-day Newfoundland. The Alberto Cantino map of 1502 shows a large island in the North Atlantic labeled as the land of the king of Portugal, giving further credence to Corte-Real's discovery of Newfoundland.

João Vaz Corte-Real

João Vaz Corte-Real may have had help; in fact he probably did. The most accepted theory about his voyage is that he was part of a joint Portuguese-Danish expedition to America. King Christian I of Denmark had sent an emissary to serve Prince Henry the Navigator. At least one historian believes that emissary was Didrik Pining, a German from Hildesheim. Since Christian and his wife were both German-born, the use of a fellow German as an emissary should not cause surprise. Pining would later serve as a Danish governor in Iceland. Pining had a long association with Hans Pothorst, another German, also from Hildesheim. A record in the Danish archives makes reference to the joint Portuguese-Danish expedition. This Letter from Carsten Grip, Burgermeister of Kiel to King Christian III of Denmark, dated March 1551—mentions the expedition of "Pining and Pothorst, the two shipmasters [who were sent] by your Royal Majesty's Grandfather, King Christian I, at the request of His Royal Majesty of Portugal with several ships to seek out new lands and countries in the north."

Historian Dr. Sofus Larsen, of the University of Copenhagen, concluded after much research that João Vaz Corte-Real accompanied Pining and Pothorst as the Portuguese representative on this joint expedition. Since the Danes controlled Iceland at the time of the voyage, 1473, and were well aware of Greenland, although settlements there had been abandoned by this time, the joint expedition to "seek out new lands" would clearly have sought those lands to the west or south of Greenland. Thus, Pining, Pothorst, and Corte-Real found or rediscovered Newfoundland, later known as the Island of Codfish and identified as Portuguese territory.

Writing in 1580, when Terra Novo do Bacalhau was clearly identified on maps as modern-day Newfoundland, Gaspar Frutuosa wrote that Corte-Real had "arrived from the Terra do Bacalhau, which he went to discover by order of the king." Although not a contemporary record, Frutuosa's statement about Corte-Real discovering Newfoundland makes it clear that the story of Corte-Real, and by extension, that of Pining and Pothorst was well-accepted by that early date.

**Tierra de Baccalaos (Land of the Codfish)
Designating Newfoundland on a Map of 1570**

After his one voyage to Newfoundland in the summer and fall of 1473, João Vaz Corte-Real never ventured back to America. However, his sons carried on the tradition. Gaspar and Miguel Corte-Real spent their youth in the court of King Manuel I of Portugal. In 1500, Gaspar received a royal charter from the king to continue the exploration of the New World northern territories. In January, 1501, King Manuel recognized the performance of one of Gaspar's crewmembers on their first voyage to Newfoundland. Letters written by two Italian spies in the Portuguese court give details about Gaspar's second voyage on which his brother

Miguel accompanied him. Alberto Cantino, spy and mapmaker, wrote to the Duke of Ferrara in October, 1501, a detailed account of Gaspar's expedition in which he reported sailing to the northern waters, encountering icebergs, describing American Indians, and other features of the modern-day Canadian coastal areas they visited.

A second spy, Pedro Pasqualigo, wrote at the same time about two of Gaspar's three caravels returning to Lisbon after their voyage to America. On board were seven men, women, and children taken from the new found lands. Pasqualigo described these Native Americans as looking like Gypsies, dressed in animal skins, and speaking an unintelligible language. He also wrote that the Portuguese explorers had determined that the land they visited was a mainland because they had sailed along its coast for about 600 miles and found no indication that it was an island. The third caravel, carrying Gaspar, disappeared in 1501, never returning to Portugal.

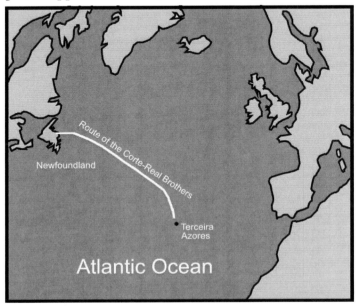

In 1502, Miguel set sail with three caravels to search for his brother and to expand the area they expected to annex for Portugal. Like his brother, Miguel vanished somewhere on this third voyage to America. There was much at stake for the Corte-Real brothers. When Gaspar had failed to return, King Manuel wrote, "and in case he does not find his brother, I declare that all the continents, or islands that he discovers, plus those found by Gaspar, be all granted to [Miguel]…."

What became of Miguel and Gaspar? The six hundred miles of coastline credited to Gaspar's discovery would have taken him to nearly the southern extent of Nova Scotia if he began at the Northern end of Newfoundland. He may have continued farther along the American coastline before sailing into historical obscurity. Miguel presumably looked for Gaspar along that same coastal route, where unaccountably he too disappeared from the historical record. A third brother, Vasco Anes Corte-Real, attempted to gain royal permission to sail off in search of his two missing brothers, but King Manuel wisely refused to allow this young man to leave Portugal on such a quest.

A forty-ton rock at Berkley, Massachusetts, may provide a clue to at least one of the places Miguel searched on his quest to find Gaspar. Dighton Rock contains an elaborate series of deeply-engraved designs that have yielded a wide variety of interpretations. The inscriptions are clearly not modern forgeries. Cotton Mather wrote about them in 1690: "…a mighty rock, on a perpendicular side whereof by a River [Taunton], which at high tide covers part of it, there are very deeply engraved, no man alive knows how or when about half a score lines, near ten foot long, and a foot and a half broad, filled with strange characters: which would suggest as odd thoughts about them that were here before us, as there are odd shapes in that elaborate monument...."

Dighton Rock, photograph dated 1893

Many of the interpretations of these engravings are unrelated to our story of the Corte-Reals and in fact provide totally unrelated texts.

Perhaps the most plausible interpretation came from a psychologist, Professor Edmund Delabarre of Brown University. Professor Delabarre devoted more than thirty years to his study of these enigmatic engravings. He initially concluded that, like an ink-blot test, the viewers could interpret them in random ways, being merely products of the viewers' fertile imaginations. But, after writing that "After prolonged and closest searching, I got so that I could find any given figure almost anywhere [on the rock]," Delabarre made an incredible discovery. He said, "... with what astonishment

… I saw in it clearly and unmistakably the date 1511. No one had ever seen it before, on rock or photograph; yet once seen, its genuine presence on the rock cannot be doubted." Looking further, Delabarre found with the date the arms of the Kingdom of Portugal and the following inscription, "Miguel Cortereal V. Dei Hic Dux Ind," which he translated to read Miguel Corte-Real, by the will of God, here leader of the Indians."

Needless to say, Professor Delabarre's conclusion regarding that part of the extensive engraving on the rock has come under scholarly criticism. Like so many ancient artifacts of epigraphy on American soil, there are as many interpretations of the Dighton Rock as there are examiners. We need not concern ourselves too much with whether Miguel Corte-Real left his inscription on this rock in modern-day Massachusetts. What we should focus on is the rather compelling story of the Portuguese re-discovery of the northeast coast of America at the end of the fifteenth century.

Some of the earliest maps from the age of exploration showing the North American continent indicate that Newfoundland had become known as the land of the codfish and tied that land to the Portugal of Corte-Real. Whereas we found no reason to believe the legend of Sir Henry Sinclair's voyage with the Zeno brothers to North America, we have found ample reason based on contemporary records to believe that João Vaz Corte-Real, in concert with Didrik Pining and Hans Pothorst, did sail to Newfoundland twenty years before Christopher Columbus sailed to southern American waters. And the record seems clear that Corte-

Real's sons followed his path to the New World to expand their father's Portuguese claim on those lands. Soon after João Vaz Corte-Real's voyage, England would stake her competing claim on the same territory.

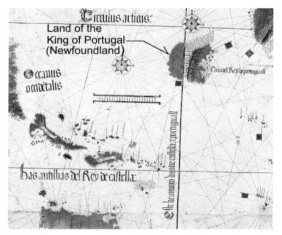

**Detail from map dated 1502 by Alberto Cantino
Showing Newfoundland as belonging to Portugal**

Chapter 13
Richard ap Merrick and Other British

""...on St John the Baptist's Day [24 June], the land of America was found by the merchants of Bristowe, in a ship of Bristowe called the Mathew." This entry appears in the Bristol calendar of events recorded in 1497. It refers to John Cabot's voyage, authorized by King Henry VII, but financed by Bristol merchants.

One of the wealthiest merchants of Bristol, England, a transplanted Welshman named Richard ap Merrick or Richard Amerike in his adopted English name, sponsored Cabot's voyage to the New World. For years during the late fifteenth century, ap Merrick had financed fishing expeditions to the rich fisheries of the Grand Banks. The English, and certainly the Basque, had discovered those fisheries by the fifteenth century, if not before.

Mythical Isle of Brasil

The mythical Isle of Brasil or Hy Brasil (also spelled Brazil) stems from Irish lore of an island shrouded in fog. Mariners could see this island only one day every seven years, but still could not reach it. The name derived from Breasal, an ancient clan of Ireland.

The island lay somewhere to the west of Ireland and medieval mapmakers as well as sixteenth-century mapmakers showed the roughly circular island lying in the Atlantic in various locations.

Brasil was also called the Isle of Truth, the Isle of Joy, the Isle of Apples, and the Isle of Fair Women. The last name perhaps gave it the most interest for mariners.

The English also looked for the mythical island of Brasil while sailing into the western ocean, and they attempted to keep their routes secret so that other countries would not discover their lucrative fishing grounds. In 1480, John Jay of Bristol sent an eighty-ton ship in search of Brasil. Jay had a regularly established trading route between England and Iceland. Unfortunately, his search for Brasil never made it past Ireland due to adverse weather conditions. In 1481, Thomas Croft partially funded a search for Brasil by two ships out of Bristol: *George* and *Trinity*. He placed forty bushels of salt aboard, perhaps indicating that the two ships would also engage in fishing in the western Atlantic. No records exist to tell us the fate of Croft's ships.

Richard ap Merrick also shipped salt to the New World, probably Newfoundland, for use ashore in processing codfish. He managed a fishing business from Bristol with his ships sailing to secret locations across the Atlantic and successfully returning with large quantities of salted codfish. For competitive reasons, ap Merrick and the other Bristol merchants wanted to maintain a monopoly on fishing the waters of the Grand Banks off Newfoundland.

According to one theory, ap Merrick gave Cabot a map showing the location of the shore-based fish processing encampment. The location bore the legend Amerike. On later versions of the map, Amerike became America, naming the territory for the man who sponsored voyages there. That would explain the rather unusual reference to America in a Bristol document dating to a period twenty years before the first known reference to America on a world map—the Waldseemuller Map of 1507.

Another Possible Origin of the Name America

Children in America are taught that America came from Amerigo Vespucci, the Florentine mariner. Actually, the best evidence, dating back to the earliest Spanish documents following Christopher Columbus, shows that part of South America—from Venezuela to Peru—was called Amaraca by the Indians of that region. At least that was what the Spaniards understood. Various spellings of Amaraca occur in Spanish documents beginning with the visit to that land by Alonzo de Ojeda, with whom Vespucci sailed in 1499.

Ojeda reported that he received friendly treatment at the hands of the Indians of Maracapana. Maracapana was also written as Amaraca Pana, the place where Columbus landed during his voyage past Trinidad and the Oronoco River a few years before Ojeda.

Map of 1562

Apparently the Indians called the general area Amaraca, and Pana meant country or region. Later visitors to the western regions of South America found that the Incas called their region Amaru Ca, and various subdivisions of Amaru Ca were identified by prefixes such as Cundin Amaraca, or And Amaraca. Subsequent spellings included the variant America.

It seems plausible that Waldseemuller labeled that area of the New World America not in honor of Amerigo Vespucci but following the Spanish name derived from what the Indians called that part of the world—America. Thus, like so many place names in America, the continental name also derives from an Indian word.

Whether fishermen in the employ of Richard ap Merrick had encampments on the shores of Newfoundland hasn't been positively established. However, it seems clear and historians generally accept that not only English fishermen, but fishermen from other nations had "discovered" that territory long before John Cabot sailed there and formally claimed the land for King Henry VII. That should not come as a surprise when we realize how long people of northern Europe had been sailing across the North Atlantic to the New World. These fishermen followed in the wake of Norse, Basque, Irish, and perhaps other nationalities.

In the end, John Cabot's voyage of 1497, five years after Columbus's first voyage to America, cemented England's claim on part of the New World. During the first three-quarters of the sixteenth century, England squandered her lead by failing to launch successful follow-up expeditions. King Henry VIII authorized John Rastell, a lawyer, playwright and printer, to lead a voyage of discovery to the New World. Rastell hired the usual bunch of sea dogs to be found frequenting the English docks and set sail for America in 1516. He made it only as far as Cork in Ireland where his crew abandoned him and took his ship off on a pirating adventure.

Soon thereafter, the Hawkins family began a three-generation period of seafaring to the New World spanning the entire sixteenth century. But their interests were purely slave trading and plunder. The progenitor, William Hawkins, began the tradition by sailing to Guinea to purchase African slaves, then transporting them to the West Indies and to

South America where he sold them to Spanish and Portuguese plantation managers.

His son John added an even more lucrative twist to this business by stealing the slaves from the Portuguese based in Guinea—sometimes even stealing the Portuguese transport ships—and then trading the slaves in the West Indies. John Hawkins became one of the most notorious English pirates of the sixteenth century and should also be remembered for giving young Francis Drake his first taste of adventure against the Spanish interests in the New World.

Richard, John's son, followed the family tradition. He fought against the Spanish Armada, sailed with Drake and participated in the rescue of Walter Ralegh's first colonists at Roanoke Island, but then attempted to duplicate Sir Francis Drake's episodes against the Spanish along the west coast of the Americas. He was captured by the Spanish and spent much of his adult life cooling his heals in Spanish prisons. When he eventually bought his freedom, he spent his remaining years ashore as mayor of Plymouth, England.

The Hawkins family demonstrates that the English had the nerve to explore the New World, but instead of planting colonies they contented themselves with plundering Spanish and Portuguese ships in search of a quicker return on their investment.

Finally in 1576, Martin Frobisher, another hero of the defense against the Armada, attempted to revitalize English interests in North America, at least as a pathway over a much-sought after Northwest Passage to Asia. But interest in a quick profit soon scuttled Frobisher's more strategic plans when he thought he found gold in the Canadian arctic, and

England became wrapped up in a foolhardy gold rush, once again failing to capitalize on their claim dating back more than three-quarters of a century to John Cabot.

A few years later, England made a series of land settlement attempts in North America. Beginning with Queen Elizabeth's patent to Sir Humphrey Gilbert in 1580, several colonial attempts took place. Gilbert failed with fatal consequences; then his half-brother, Walter Ralegh, made two better organized, but ultimately unsuccessful attempts to secure a permanent place in North America for the English. By 1590, Ralegh had lost interest in North America, for all practical purposes.

Success finally came when a business venture called the Virginia Company of London delivered a little more than one hundred men and boys to Jamestown, Virginia in May, 1607. From that point on, England would have control—albeit tenuous at first—over most of North America. Spain and France would contend against England through the seventeenth century for dominion over North America. By the beginning of the nineteenth century, the new United States of America would gain control over much of North America except Canada and Central America.

Epilog

In 1492 Columbus sailed the ocean blue. That's true, but we know that far from being the first discoverer of the Americas, Christopher Columbus was its last discoverer.

Perhaps coming last makes him more important. He deserves credit for inaugurating a new European interest for the invasion of America in unprecedented proportions. Following Columbus, Spain and Portugal established permanent settlements in North, Central, and South America. They sent thousands of their citizens to the New World to hold, develop, and expand their dominion over those territories. In addition to their own citizens, they sent thousands of captive African slaves to assist in their exploitation of the valuable resources of the New World. Spain in particular came to dominate Western Europe in the sixteenth century due to the continuous stream of wealth acquired in the New World and carried back to the old Phoenician port of Cadiz (Gades).

Apart from the Scandinavian settlement of Iceland, and for a time Greenland, Europe had failed to send a critical mass of settlers to the Americas. The fleeting contacts with Native Americans by Chinese, Phoenicians, Vikings, Israelites, Irish, Welsh, Libyan, and perhaps African and Polynesian mariners left important genetic and cultural traces across the Americas, but those traces became fully assimilated among the Native Americans. The American Indian cultures remained dominant, perhaps containing cultural echoes of those past contacts, but absorbing those contacts in uniquely Indian ways.

When the Spanish arrived with Columbus and in later waves of invasion, the American Indian way of life became overrun by the foreign conquistadors. Indians succumbed to diseases they had not encountered before. The greatest loss of Indian populations came about not by combat with Spanish or Portuguese soldiers, but with an invisible enemy for which they had no resistance. The survivors became subservient to the conquering Spaniards first, and later to conquerors from Portugal, France, and Britain.

As is often the case, isolated and marginalized Indians and African slaves banded together in many locales to attempt to maintain their independent way of life. Thus into the modern era, indigenous peoples of the Americas incorporated additional genetic elements into their dwindling populations. The Native American populations that remain today must carry an incredible blend of genetic traces beginning at the end of the last Ice Age and continuing into the modern era. That they have been able to maintain their rich culture, their ancient religious beliefs, and their tribal identity in the face of this foreign onslaught is astounding.

Modern genetic science will eventually find in the DNA of Native Americans a positive record of all of the human migrations, accidental and purposeful, that contributed to the blending of cultures that occurred over about eighteen thousand years in America. That record will further substantiate the accounts of the many incursions into the New World of people outlined in this book. Until then, we can continue to speculate about if, when, and how people from Asia, Europe, Africa, and Polynesia came to America to make up the people Christopher Columbus called "Indians."

Image Credits

P. 5—Photograph of Eskimo in a Umiak at Cape Prince of Wales, Alaska, by Edward S. Curtis, digital ID ct20053, Library of Congress.

P. 7—Path of the Solutreans, map by author.

P. 11—Ancient Susquehanna River Course, map by author.

P. 33—Comparison of Solutrean and Clovis Points, drawing by author.

P. 35—Location of Calico Hills in California, map by author

P. 36—Monte Verde and Pedra Furada Archaeological Sites, map by author.

P. 37—Seal Level Rise Since the Ice Age, graph by author

P. 38—The Bering Land Bridge Between Asia and North America, map by author.

P. 40—The Ice-Free Corridor through North America, map by author.

P. 42—Indian Dugout Canoe, cropped from Image 60, Das sechste Theil Americae oder Der Historien Hieron. Benzo das dritte Buch. Darinnen erzehlet wirt, wie die Spanier die..., published in Oppenheim, 1620. The Kraus Collection of Sir Francis Drake, Library of Congress.

P. 45—Archaeological Sites of Red Paint People in Maine, map by author.

P. 46—Typical Red Paint Culture Artifacts, drawing by author.

P. 48—Drawing of Rock Carving Depicting a Boat at Brandskog, Sweden, drawing by author.

P. 50—Emperor Shun, Wikimedia Commons, from *Outlines of Chinese History,* by Li Ung Bin.

P. 51—Drawing based on a 1763 copy of a Chinese Map of 1418, drawing by author.

P. 55—Quetzalcoatl, drawing by author based on image in Codex Telleriano-Remensis.

P. 60—King Solomon on His Throne, Wikipedia image file.

P. 61—Drawing of Phoenician Ship, based on bas relief carving on a sarcophagus at the National Museum of Beirut, drawing by author.

P. 62—Phoenician Alphabet, table by author.

P. 63—Typical Indian Petroglyphs of the Southwest, photo-mosaic by author.

P. 64—The Los Luñas Rock Inscription, drawing by author.

P. 67—Location of Los Luñas, New Mexico, map by author.

P. 69—A Portion of the Petroglyphs at Peterborough, Ontario, Canada, drawing by author.

P. 70—Tifinag Alphabet, table by author.

P. 75—Ivory Baton-Shaped Artifact from Grave Creek, drawing by author.

P. 76—Grave Creek Stone, drawing by author.

P. 78—Ogham Alphabet, table by author.

P. 78—Ogham Stone Near Dún Aengus Fort, Aran Isles, Ireland, photograph by author.

P. 80—Bat Creek Stone, *12th Annual Report of the Bureau of American Ethnology to the Secretary of the Smithsonian Institution 1890-1891, 1894; Report on the mound Explorations of the Bureau of*

Ethnology, photograph contained therein, translation indications added by author.

P. 82—Plaque from Father Crespi's Collection with Libyan Inscriptions, drawing by author.

P. 83—14th Century BCE Assyrian or Hittite Bas Relief, photograph from Wikimedia Commons, original sculpture at the Louvre in Paris, France.

P. 86—St. Brendan Depicted in a 15th Century German Manuscript, *Brendan de Clonfert, Manuscriptum translationis germanicae,* ca. 1460, Wikimedia Commons.

P. 90—St. Brendan's Isle, detail from map by Abraham Ortelius, *Theatrum orbis terrarum, Novo Orbis,* dated 1570, Map Division, Library of Congress.

P. 91—Tim Severin's *Brendan,* drawing by author.

P. 93—The Course of the *Brendan,* map by author.

P. 96—Eric the Red in Fanciful Armor, frontispiece from *Gronlandia,* by Arngrimur Jonsson, 1668, Wikimedia Commons.

P. 97—Eric the Red Discovers Greenland, Illustration from *Harper's Weekly,* v. 19, p. 780, September, 1875, digital image cph 3a06616, Prints and Photographs Division, Library of Congress.

P. 101—Leif Eriksson Discovers America, International Publishing Co., ca. 1911, print by Christian Krohg, digital image cph 3a06612, Prints and Photographs Division, Library of Congress.

P. 108—Remains of Viking Longhouse and Viking artifacts, photo-mosaic by author.

P. 110—Location of Viking Settlement Found in Newfoundland, map by author.

P. 121—Madoc's route, drawing by author.

P. 123—The Journey of Prince Madoc's Welsh Settlers, map by author.

P. 127—A Mandan Woman in One of Their Unusual "Bull Boats," *Mandan Bull Boat*, photograph by Edward S. Curtis, digital ID cph 3a55033, Library of Congress.

P. 131—A Portrait of George Catlin by William Fisk done in 1849, Wikimedia Commons.

P. 135—Estotiland and Drogio Shown on a Map of the Atlantic in 1570, detail from map by Abraham Ortelius, *Theatrum orbis terrarum, Novo Orbis,* dated 1570, Map Division, Library of Congress.

P. 136—A 1793 Copy of the Zeno Map of 1558, from *Priisskrift om Grønlands Østerbygds sande Beliggenhed*, by Henrich Peter von Eggers, 1793.

P. 141—The Westford Knight Carving As Seen by Sir Henry Sinclair Advocates, drawing by author.

P. 142—Chinese Ship of the 15th Century, early 17th century Chinese woodblock print thought to represent Zheng He's ships, Wikimedia Commons.

P. 144—Ming Emperor Zhu Di, Wikimedia Commons.

P. 145—A Giraffe, the Chinese Mythical Qilin, from a copy of a Ming Dynasty (1414) painting, Wikimedia Commons.

P. 146—Detail From the Fra Mauro Map, Fra Mauro's World Map of 1450, Wikimedia Commons.

P. 147—The Known Route of Zheng He's Voyages, map by author.

P. 148—Kangnido Map of 1402, Wikimedia Commons.

P. 150—Ming Era Brass Presentation Disk Found by R. W. Shinnick, drawing by author.

P. 157—Fifteenth Century Portuguese Ships Sailing to India, detail from map by Diego Guitérrez, *Americae sive qvartae orbis partis nova et exactissima description*, dated 1562, digital image g3290 ct000342, Map Division, Library of Congress.

P. 159—João Vaz Corte-Real, Wikimedia Commons.

P. 161—Tierra de Baccalaos (Land of Codfish), detail from map by Abraham Ortelius, *Theatrum orbis terrarum, Novo Orbis*, dated 1570, Map Division, Library of Congress.

P. 162—Route of the Corte-Real Brothers, map by author.

P. 164—Dighton Rock, Photograph dated 1893, Wikimedia Commons.

P. 166—Detail From Map Dated 1502 by Alberto Cantino, Wikimedia Commons.

 P. 169—Inset Map Showing Maraca Pana, detail from map by Diego Guitérrez, *Americae sive qvartae orbis partis nova et exactissima description*, dated 1562, digital image g3290 ct000342, Map Division, Library of Congress.

Index

Index

Index

Index

Index

Index

Index

Index

Index

Index